MW00338284

Bible Interpretations

Second Series

October 4 - December 27, 1891

Bible
Interpretations

Second Series

John 11:21-44 to John 21:1-14

These Bible Interpretations were given during the
early eighteen nineties at the Christian Science Theological Seminary at Chicago, Illinois. This Seminary
was independent of the First Church of Christ Scientist in Boston, Mass.

By

Emma Curtis Hopkins

*President of the Christian Science Theological Semi-
nary at Chicago, Illinois*

WISEWOMAN PRESS

Bible Interpretations: Second Series

By Emma Curtis Hopkins

© WiseWoman Press

Managing Editor: Michael Terranova

ISBN 978-0-945385-52-3

WiseWoman Press

Portland, OR 97217

www.wisewomanpress.com

www.emmacurtishopkins.com

CONTENTS

Foreword

By Rev. Natalie R. Jean

I have read many teachings by Emma Curtis Hopkins, but the teachings that touch the very essence of my soul are her Bible Interpretations. There are many books written on the teachings of the Bible, but none can touch the surface of the true messages more than these Bible interpretations. With each word you can feel and see how Spirit spoke through Emma. The mystical interpretations take you on a wonderful journey to Self Realization.

Each passage opens your consciousness to a new awareness of the realities of life. The illusions of life seem to disappear through each interpretation. Emma teaches that we are the key that unlocks the doorway to the light that shines within. She incorporates ideals of other religions into her teachings, in order to understand the commonalities, so that there is a complete understanding of our Oneness. Emma opens our eyes and mind to a better today and exciting future.

Emma Curtis Hopkins, one of the Founders of New Thought teaches us to love ourselves, to speak our Truth, and to focus on our Good. My life has moved in wonderful directions because of her teachings. I know the only thing that can move me in this world is God. May these interpretations guide you to a similar path and may you truly remember that "There Is Good For You and You Ought to Have It."

Introduction

Emma Curtis Hopkins was born in 1849 in Killingsly, Connecticut. She passed on April 8, 1925. Mrs. Hopkins had a marvelous education and could read many of the worlds classical texts in their original language. During her extensive studies she was always able to discover the Universal Truths in each of the world's sacred traditions. She quotes from many of these teachings in her writings. As she was a very private person, we know little about her personal life. What we do know has been gleaned from other people or from the archived writings we have been able to discover.

Emma Curtis Hopkins was one of the greatest influences on the New Thought movement in the United States. She taught over 50,000 people the Universal Truth of knowing "God is All there is." She taught many of founders of early New Thought, and in turn these individuals expanded the influence of her teachings. All of her writings encourage the student to enter into a personal relationship with God. She presses us to deny anything except the Truth of this spiritual Presence in every area of our lives. This is the central focus of all her teachings.

The first six series of Bible Interpretations were presented at her seminary in Chicago, Illinois. The remaining Series', probably close to thirty, were printed in the Inter Ocean Newspaper in Chicago. Many of the lessons are no longer available for various reasons. It is the intention of WiseWoman Press to publish as many of these Bible Interpretations as possible. Our hope is that any missing lessons will be found or directed to us.

I am very honored to join the long line of people that have been involved in publishing Emma Curtis Hopkins's Bible Interpretations. Some confusion exists as to the numbering sequence of the lessons. In the early 1920's many of the lessons were published by the Highwatch Fellowship. Inadvertently the first two lessons were omitted from the numbering system. Rev. Joanna Rogers has corrected this mistake by finding the first two lessons and restoring them to their rightful place in the order. Rev. Rogers has been able to find many of the missing lessons at the International New Thought Alliance archives in Mesa, Arizona. Rev. Rogers painstakingly scoured the archives for the missing lessons as well as for Mrs. Hopkins other works. She has published much of what was discovered. WiseWoman Press is now publishing the correctly numbered series of the Bible Interpretations.

In the early 1940's, there was a resurgence of interest in Emma's works. , At that time, Highwatch Fellowship began to publish many of her writings, and it was then that *High Mysticism*, her seminal work was published. Previously, the material contained in High Mysticism was only available as individual lessons and was brought together in book form for the first time. Although there were many errors in these first publications and many Bible verses were incorrectly quoted, I am happy to announce that WiseWoman Press is now publishing *High Mysticism* in the a corrected format. This corrected form was scanned faithfully from the original, individual lessons.

The next person to publish some of the Bible Lessons was Rev. Marge Flotron from the Ministry of Truth International in Chicago, Illinois. She published the Bible Lessons as well as many of Emma's other works. By her initiative, Emma's writings were brought to a larger audience when DeVorss & Company, a longtime publisher of Truth Teachings, took on the publication of her key works.

In addition, Dr. Carmelita Trowbridge, founding minister of The Sanctuary of Truth in Alhambra, California, inspired her assistant minister, Rev. Shirley Lawrence, to publish many of Emma's works, including the first three series of Bible Interpretations. Rev. Lawrence created mail order courses for many of these Series. She has graciously passed on any information she had, in order to assure that these works continue to inspire individuals and groups who are called to further study of the teachings of Mrs. Hopkins.

Finally, a very special acknowledgement goes to Rev Natalie Jean, who has worked diligently to retrieve several of Emma's lessons from the Library of Congress, as well as libraries in Chicago. Rev. Jean hand-typed many of the lessons she found on microfilm. Much of what she found is on her website, www.highwatch.net.

It is with a grateful heart that I am able to pass on these wonderful teachings. I have been studying dear Emma's works for fifteen years. I was introduced to her writings by my mentor and teacher, Rev. Marcia Sutton. I have been overjoyed with the results of delving deeply into these Truth Teachings.

In 2004, I wrote a Sacred Covenant entitled "Resurrecting Emma," and created a website, www.emmacurtishopkins.com. The result of creating this covenant and website has brought many of Emma's works into my hands and has deepened my faith in God. As a result of my love for these works, I was led to become a member of Wise-Woman Press and to publish these wonderful teachings. God is Good.

My understanding of Truth from these divinely inspired teachings keeps bringing great Joy, Freedom, and Peace to my life.

Dear reader; It is with an open heart that I offer these works to you, and I know they will touch you as they have touched me. Together we are living in the Truth that God is truly present, and living for and through each of us.

The greatest Truth Emma presented to us is "My Good is my God, Omnipresent, Omnipotent and Omniscient."

Rev. Michael Terranova

WiseWoman Press

Vancouver, Washington, 2010

LESSON I

MARY AND MARTHA

John 11:21-44

"Martha" represents the preachers and active workers in religious bodies since ever there was any teaching in the world concerning the Being and office of God. These have ever asserted that God is Omnipresence and without flaw or imperfection of any kind, absolutely good.

At the same time they have been telling of many grievous things happening, as earthquakes, death, loss, which could not possibly have transpired: if God's mercy had been shown forth, or if God had not been the "absence of the good" then and there. Such discrepancies of statements as that God, the absolute Good, is Omnipresence and "the absence of good" have necessitated "Martha's" placing Deity on a throne somewhere in the far spaces, as a Being with uncertain moods, who might and might not reward and punish, according to petitions.

The truth is that God is Principle. The principle of goodness. Goodness is best. To do the best you can is to serve the best, and the best, as a principle will reward you. "His reward is in His hand." Just as surely as you do the best you can the best will come to you. This is the principle of righteousness. To trust the sure action of this principle will demonstrate the sight of the best speedily. Not to trust its intelligent action retards the sight of the best.

And the best you could imagine, and "greater" will come to you by trusting that, no matter what you accomplish, your motive being good, the best is sure to come to you. This is Principle.

It is either worth while to trust to the righteousness of your motive to bring you out right, or it is not worth while. The sooner you make up your mind whether you will trust to the motive to bring to pass, or to the method of action, the better for your peace of mind. This is the chief tenet of Christian science doctrine — not the method, but the motive. The good motive is the Christ presence — Christ principle — never absent, always working. To do the very best you can is sure to bring you out right, an unfailing, unalterable law.

Suppose that you have had some noble idea of what was right to do under certain circumstances, as, for instance, that by some special attention, you could bring forth the genius so near to the surface of the loud woman or the coarse man? You must give them your kind support and friendly counsel. You know this to be right. But some of the people you love best withdraw their acquaintance and friendship on account of your new comrades. You must trust that the simple being in the right will be your satisfactory demonstration. The best will come of it, because you did your best. Trust it and the demonstration thereof will be speedy.

It is not a choice of friends, though their sophistry might put it that way, it is a question of what is right, and you must trust it to act.

When Martha's brother was sick they did the best they could, and that best was the Christ's presence. If they trusted it they would have seen it work whether Jesus was present or not. Lazarus would have got well; it was not to trust that Lazarus would get well, nor to any method of hot or cold applications, drugs or poultices, but to trust their motive which prompted every action. The successful healers often do very poorly according to the world's ideas of methods. They succeed because they do trust to their ideas of right. The difference between a small trader and a merchant prince is that the small trader looks anxiously to his pints and quarts and wonders how they will act with him next, while the merchant prince knows of the wheat crops of the world, who owns the ships, and what winds are blowing, to determine the prices in advance. That you are in the right must sustain you. That your highest ideal of what is right must he carried out by you — must be your principle of action.

This was the doctrine of Jesus Christ: "Have Faith in God." God is Good. Good is right. Right is best. A lively confidence in the success of the doctrine of doing your best will be like the confidence of Jesus Christ. If a man should set out that he could feed all the world's hungry children he could do it if he loved the idea enough to persevere in practicing it. People might call him a fanatic or an idealist, and prophesy that he would break his neck on his ideals, but back of him would be the infinite bounty of the right idea.

Two women were conversing about giving forth freely their highest ideas to the people. One said she thought it a conservation of energy to keep your original ideas to yourself. Original ideas were not plentiful. People did things over and over, and great ideas would soon give out if you gave them forth freely. The other said that she felt like a clear pane of glass through which bright ideas went freely till she tried to hoard them, then she felt like a pane that had gathered dust.

The first one not only did not bless the people, but got into a confused and timid state of mind with a sick body. The second one grew clearer and clearer and blessed and cheered and delighted the lowest as well as the highest, besides having a body as healthy as her mind. Both knew that it is right to believe in the bounty of God as unfailing. One trusted the principle, the other did not.

4

Mahomet was asked to put away Cadijah for a younger and fairer woman. "No! By Allah! She made me," he said.

Napoleon was asked to put away Josephine. "The star is mine, Napoleon," she reminded him. He yielded to the temptation, however, and from that hour his decline began. The days find his name slipping from the praise of men, while the years increase the millions who honor Mahomet. There is such a close and vital connection between standing for the principle of right and failing it!

"Even now," said Martha. The church always says that if only some one had been on hand to trust the God principle. Why did not the church herself have the faith? It is a working principle. Why not exercise it? Jesus tarried away, hoping they would realize that the truth of God is never absent as a live-saving certainty. They had heard Him tell that they must speak true words as intensely as they feared or grieved. Fear and grief are intense feelings to which the world sets fearful and grievous words. Thus the fruits are grievous. No matter how much grieved you are, never say, "I am grieved." The grief is a fertile soil for such words, and grievous things come up quickly to you if you speak such appropriate words. Say, instead, "In my idea of good there is no grief." A wonderful change of mind will take place, which will be a forerunner of good tidings.

Martha assured Jesus that she expected Lazarus to rise at the "last day." Why at the last day?

Why not now? "Now is the accepted time" with the Good. A hospital patient was told to wait till after death for her cure by pious physicians, but one who believed that Lazarus ought to be raised today cured her this side the tomb, and she rejoices to know that there is a difference between a great idea believed in and doubted.

"I am the Resurrection," said Jesus. Anybody who believes in the life and goodness of the principle he advocates will demonstrate it. He will be so at one with the principle he advocates that he will not know the difference between himself and it. Jesus advocated the power of a right confidence to change the particles of our bodies into a transcendent substance incapable evermore of seeming to die.

"Believest thou this?" Martha told Him that the expected Messiah would do this. This idea of a Messiah had got mixed with the sight of the Roman conquerors. They wanted someone who would trample on the living necks of their enemies till they were dead. But this Messiah who had come in answer to the prayers of the saints had refused to take away life, "I came that you might have life . . . more abundantly." I did not come for your honors, your social distinctions, your favors; I came to tell you how to trust God for your bread and home and health.

Then "Mary" came out and wept and spoke exactly as "Martha" had. "Mary" represents the modest laymen who always do exactly as the

6

preachers and bold workers tell them to do, but who have a better trust than their leaders. It is their very simplicity of faith that leads them to do as they are told, but when they hear a principle they love it and verily wish "Martha" would let them act out their deepest convictions.

Then Jesus "groaned." He was indignant. He was to what extremity bondage to doubt of the good would lead. He spake within Himself some bold, good words to match the intense feeling. When your environments grieve or anger you, do not let your thoughts run down their gloomy track, but rise with the clear utterance of the conviction that has never been whispered by you. This is it: "there is good for me and I ought to have it." The bird says this and flies hither and yon, and the stones look up and around for the good they know is theirs by right. The galley slave believes this and the prince reels through the banquet halls to find it. Just as soon as the idea has utterance, that which is for you:

"Will rise the hills and swim the sea

To fall, fair sunshine, full on thee."

The stenographer at her keys and the sewing girls at her dull task must speak forth this long-chained conviction, speak it boldest when the hours are blackest. The streetcar man and the cash boy — kings are they all, and into their inheritance they begin to come with the utterance of the confidence of their hearts: "There is good for me and I ought to have it." There is infinite fullness of good for you, child.

Roll away the stone of belief in future good. Say, "Now." Don't be afraid to speak intensely; "I do not believe there is any power in the universe can keep me away from my good." "Martha" objects to hopes being raised and says that if the child you pray for should live he might grow up a drunkard, or that prosperity might spoil him.

Jews believed that an angel dropped a bit of gall on the people whom death had covered. Death is nothing but the fruit of doubt. This is the preaching of resignation to disappointed hopes. Don't you be resigned to evil of any kind. Throw it out of your faith. Refuse traditions. Refuse to hear anybody who says the worst is good.

There are beautiful ways for God to work. Do not believe that a railway accident has harmed your family though all the papers say so. Get their rooms and table ready. Roll away the stone. Give thanks that you have faith in the action of the good and do not believe in mixing your ideas of good with any kind of evil. Then call to them to come home. The low lands will answer, "Coming" and the uplands will cry, "We come." For omnipotent love hears the prayer of faith. "By faith the dead are raised." Faith is only confidence in the action of a principle as sure as mathematics.

You believe that water will run down hill. Well, "Let the Lord be thy confidence. He will not suffer thy feet to be taken." Loose Lazarus from his grave clothes when he is risen. Loose the maimed bodies of your loved ones from the murmurs that they are not returned home as sound as they went away. Loose your partial cure which came in answer to prayer from your complaining that it is not all restored.

"Praise God for what has come so far forth.

Hold fast what thou hast,

Then they will soon be "every whit whole,"

The morn swings incense silver gray.

The night is past!

No priest, no church can bar its way,

The night is past.

The spirit and the bride say come.

Come boldly up and drink, thirsty heart."

October 4, 1891

LESSON II

GLORY OF CHRIST

John 12:20-36

In last Sunday's lesson you ought to have read "There is good for me and I ought to have it" in that line which said, "This is good," etc. The sewing girl at her task and the cash boy running at orders of another human being must not say, "This is good," for that is the old teaching of resignation to what we do not like. The white stone of revealing is, "There is good for me and I ought to have it." Keep this omnipresent, omnipotent truth going in your mind and you will be a magnet for success and joy.

Also you must read, "grief is a fertile soil" instead of "futile evil," for if you put a strong truth into your feeling of grief the union of the word and the feeling will make a fertile soil for a great good to grow up in. For Grief is the call for a bold statement of faith in the good.

This lesson tells you what to do when, having espoused a great principle or determined to cast yourself upon your righteous motive to take you safely through, you find yourself persecuted and lightly esteemed by the people among whom you have cast your lot, and are invited by another class of people who recognize your greatness and your goodness to come and be identified with them.

The Jewish church was the chosen field of Jesus. It held Him as a bright, headstrong young fellow who, though a carpenter, might have done well and been considered of some account if He had not got into such strange notions.

The Greeks who came to Him at this time came as representatives of the worship of externals carried to the highest ultimates.

Many thoughtful Greeks had felt that there was something radically wrong about the worship of beings with the appetites and passions and frailties of mankind, even though such beings did inspire the genius of a Phidias; so they had turned to the Jewish worship of the God of Abraham, Isaac, and Jacob.

The Jehovah of Abraham was the provider. There should be no lack when this God was trusted. The Jehovah of Isaac was the defender. There should no ill befall when this God was trusted. The Jehovah of Jacob was the principle of righteousness. There should be no failure where this God was trusted. Jehovah-jireh (Jehovah will provide). Jehovah-nissi (Jehovah is my banner).

11

Jehovah-tsid kenu (Jehovah my righteousness). One Lord and His Name One.

To cast yourself on the Good as your Provider would be sure bounty. To cast yourself on the Good as your Defense would be sure protection. To cast yourself on the Good as your Rewarder would make every good action and word its own justification.

This principle seemed, indeed, a more reasonable lawgiver than Olympian Jove, with his ivory limbs, gold draperies and eyes of jewels, or Minerva with her immortal beauty. A principle with unvarying laws was greater than an unreliable god of the clouds. This was the way the Greeks felt.

To be a Daniel with the understanding of this Being of power was more worthy than to be a Phidias. For Phidias had no safety from lions' jaws and angry kings, while Daniel was safe as a babe in its cradle though such terrors folded him.

One step towards independent thinking always compels the next step and makes it easy. It is such a joy to find yourself thinking, as is reasonable to yourself instead of, as somebody has told you. A Universalist who was snubbed by the Methodists, Baptists, Congregationists a few years ago, is sure to take every new thought and look it straight in the face.

So the proselyted or converted Greek went to see Jesus, the young Jew who was faring so savagely at the hands of the high churchmen. They were interested in His extraordinary claims, making Himself equal with God, and telling even the common fishermen that they were as great as Himself. They were attracted by the reasonableness of the doctrine that one may be so one with truth that he calls himself Truth — may be so in love with Goodness that he is lost in the omnipresence, omnipotence, omniscience of Goodness.

They recognized the teaching as exactly adapted to fascinate the philosophical Greeks, as an ethical culture with spiritual potentialities. So they formally invited Him to be a recognized teacher of spiritual ethics. Philip and Andrew presented their claims as a formal committee. Philip was the one who told Jesus that there were 5,000 people and that 500 penny-worth of bread would not feed them. Andrew was the one who counted up that five barley loaves and two fishes were all they had on hand.

So Philip, true to his character, told what a noble way of living his Master was worthy of; how highly His genius and talents would be appreciated; what wonderful libraries, handsome estates, and dignities would be His if He would go among the Gentiles. Why He might be even more highly regarded than Apollonious of Tyana — the companion of Princes.

Andrew reminded Him that there were so many teachers of high repute among the Jews that even though He (Jesus) might have a doctrine greater and truer than them all, yet He would stand no chance in His lifetime of being anything among them; said they had been treated dreadfully and had made only a very few converts. It would serve the Jews right to leave them. But Jesus knew He was the answer to the prayers of the pious prophets and noble mothers of Israel, whose hearts had been true to the true God in the midst of temptations.

They had been the only ones to hold on to the Being of love and goodness unchangeable. The promise had been that ten men out of all nations should lay hold of the skirts of the Jews, for they had always had God with them. He knew this promise and knew His doctrine as its fulfillment.

He called it His glory to stand there in His lot until the end of the days. He recognized the treatment of the Jews as the greatest proclamation possible to call attention to His teachings. Nothing tempted Him from the sight of this law whereby all nations should be beckoned on. He hastened the coming crucifixion by saying, *"The hour is now come."*

He knew the law of the hastening power of those words, which state that a thing is already come to pass when it is not yet seen. An epileptic man cured himself in a few minutes, forever, by ecstasy: "Praise God I am healed!" when he had not any intimation of being healed, but had this law of saying that it is finished before you see it so.

Jesus did exactly the same way on the cross. Before it was apparently finished He said, "It is finished." He never saw the transactions going on with their eyes for a moment. It was all success and glory to Him. The Christian scientist who is true to his affirmation that the good is working with him and through him and by him and for him, does not see or hear anything but good, while the rest see evil. He will not let his idea of good get any mixture of evil.

Why the international committee, (Clerics who produced the Bible Quotations for each year's use in churches all over the world.) chose as the title of this lesson "Death" when it is all about Glory is a wonder. Jesus Himself was prophesying glorification, but they say He was prophesying death. God cannot be anything but glorified. Remember this. He here tells them by this mention of the grain of corn that unless we put our living truth right down boldly into the hard, ugly experiences of everyday life and let that truth defy and deny and push away the material seemings to show its omnipotence, we shall be forced to go out of this world without demonstrating what great power over environments we have. He explained that the world around us must show back to us our highest ideals, but unless we boldly proclaim the truth it will not. We must announce a principle of action and live it out. Hating the temporary notions offered by emoluments and dignities we are most prosperous by loving our principle.

If you were asked to rent your corner block to a rum seller for three times the rent a Methodist or Baptist bookseller would offer you, you would not look at the first offer though you had not enough to pay the taxes and needed the money apparently. Shall you sell the land to the man when you know it will ruin him because it has depreciated and he does not know it? Can you trust the principle of righteousness to bring you out right? Shall you overcharge the man who does not know prices? One way is keeping your life; the other is hiding it. Earthly life or ways count for nothing. Principle is everything.

"Shall I yield to these offers?" Jesus asked. "Never! I came to show men how to live the principle of righteousness — not by donating large gifts to orphan's homes, nor by building charity institutions, though these are well enough, but by honorably and justly dealing with the fathers of those children."

"It is not by sheltering My physical body nor by protecting My name that I can show a man how to stand steadfast to his highest ideals, but by demonstrating the power of the spirit of man over every sort and kind of circumstance, I could have saved myself from every indignity to which I have been subject, I know the law of my ownership of all the earth. Forty days in the wilderness I studied this question for the nations; for the beggar, the prince, the priest, I know but one law."

Here he felt the principle of righteousness so strong within Him that it was the voice of God. All good men and women from Moses down through Gautama and the saints have heard a living Voice speak when they have been stirred to the foundations of their being. This Voice proclaimed that It had always and would forever honor Itself when proclaimed. You do not need to fight for a great Truth. You have only to proclaim it. You need not fight evil. Speak Truth and evil falters and fails. Evil is a lie. Truth kills lies by its own quality. Evil fought is like the flinty rock that resists the iron wedges driven by sledges, but yields to the wet wooden wedge as it swells within its bosom.

"Sharper than steel is the sword of the Spirit,

Swifter than arrows the word of the Truth is,

Stronger than anger is love and subdueth."

Some thought this Voice was an angel. Others said it thundered. When you live up to your highest conception of right some will say you are a good person, but deluded. Others will say you do everything to show off your personality and get to yourself praise of mankind. He told them that the judgment of the world was now going to be that He was crucified; that His body was stolen and His doctrine was a failure because it would not demonstrate His own safety.

But He knew that whenever this deed was mentioned men would ask wherefore He was lifted up, and then when it was explained that it was

17

because He had preached the power of God the Good Spirit and the powerlessness of evil in every form that these men would say He was right and they again would lift up the cross in their way as He in His. The down beam of the cross is the saying; "There is no power in evil." The cross beam is, "The Good is all power." This shall be preached until every knee shall bow and every tongue confess the glory of Truth.

He told them to believe in Truth while it was among them. Whoever preaches the right of way of Truth and Goodness, he is right. Listen to him. Whoever says man and God are ONE, hear him, for mind is as great as it has courage to declare itself, and demonstrates its greatness to the extent it can lose itself in its declarations.

Do not believe in persecutions or death or failure. They are not your portion. You have a light within that enables you to know when a preacher is in the right. Walk according to the highest you know and your light will increase. The temperance women, who, in their zeal for the rights of the home, got those pictures of diseased stomachs into the schools to show the effects of alcohol, have seen the strongest light of judgment shine which says that as a musician would have only perfect tones before his pupils so the teacher of life should describe only noble lives else our children will get like what they have heard described.

"Vice seen too oft, familiar with her face, we first endure, then pity, then embrace." The good is life described as unchanging, unending goodness. The eyesight and hearing will not fail when life is described.

Health teachings stimulate health. When this law of Truth is the light of the mind, the cities shall not need the sun, for God is the light. The material sun but symbolizes the light, which the principle of righteousness makes within us. Our idea of good is our LIGHT.

October 11, 1891

LESSON III

GOOD IN SACRIFICE

John 13:1-17

When one proposes to make sacrifice of himself in any way he must be sure to ask himself the question, "What good am I doing by this action?" For unless there is some actual good to be attained or achieved by doing menial or servile tasks it is the misuse of talent to put it to doing what others are better adapted to doing. Talent along any line should exercise itself to its highest expansion along that line and not intrude itself upon the domain of another without righteous cause.

Out of the action of Jesus Christ in washing the feet of His companions, a religious ceremony of washing feet has come to pass among a certain sect. But if He meant by His action simply to teach a state of mind and not a ceremonial to be observed, we had better understand the mental lesson rather than the best method of washing our neighbor's feet.

Some people think that if we keep up the ordinance of the "Lord's Supper" we ought to keep up the ceremonial of washing feet. Some think that if we believe in the literal bodily healings of Jesus we ought to believe in the fastings He practiced as duties incumbent.

In any case if we have made up our mind that this Teacher was exactly right in everything He did, we ought to find out how much indeed of the letter of His life it is our duty and privilege to perform. If He meant that it is possible to get into a state of mind which will be a healing potency to others; and into a state of mind where though of royal heritage we are willing to do the most servile services for our neighbors; and into a state of mind where spiritual ecstasy is wisdom and takes the place of eating; and that these states of mind are the desideratum of life, why we are one and all eager to attain unto them.

They intimate powers and immunities which are the *summutn bonum* (greatest good) of human hopes. Was it the fasting, was it the eating, was it the washing, which He was teaching? Or was it mental status?

He said Himself that the flesh (or material performance) counted as nothing. ("Profiteth nothing,") i.e., that it is sure to be right if the animus is right. There has been a great criticism of the idea that the motive is the justification of the action, as much as to say that a man with a very good motive might be loose in his conduct. No.

That is exactly what he could not be. Right motive
makes right action.

The right motive is the conviction in the heart
that right is right. And this conviction of right has
never been secured till it demonstrates right actions. "Conviction is not, properly speaking;
conviction till it develops itself into action." One
says that this law of righteous motive will not
work in daily affairs. Would the righteous choose
to have a set of china fired without breaking, keep
the china pieces from breaking if there were air
bubbles under the glazing?

Most certainly. You would become so intuitive
by the idea steadily held that you must do every
thing well which you attempt to do, that you would
discover a process of firing imperfect china safely
and another process of perfecting imperfect china.
There is a law of right in itself, which conducts to
right actions. It is metaphysical to think only of
the right itself. It is the highest schoolmaster.

Joshua did not know the first thing about that
law of a body resounding when its keynote is
struck. But Joshua was so sure he was in the right
that he thought out a quick way to sound the keynote to the walls of Jericho till they tumbled down.
The missionaries on the desolate island were so
sure of being in the right and were so confident in
the power of goodness of their God that they flung
the American flag to the breeze when the natives
were about to slay them. This reminded the natives what nation backed the missionaries. They

never thought of the flag till they had prayed to God. Joshua never thought of the rams' horns till he prayed to the same God.

This God unto whom they prayed for such assistance will help us in the simplest maters. Nothing is too low or ignoble for God to be the worker. "Who sweeps a room as to his God makes all the act divine."

Joseph Cook said that Lionel Beale was wishing somebody would get back into the secret of natural law and upset what seems to have so much power against. The secret is understanding of God. The feet symbolize understanding. We must keep our understanding clear and speak such words as will wash or clear the understanding of our neighbors.

There are certain words, which the mind can use that have the effect of clarifying it. The judgment can he trained to be exactly reliable by these thoughts. Jesus Christ taught the ideas that act so powerfully with the judgment.

Judas Iscariot had had an idea put into his mind that dulled or hid his judgment. This idea was that a sum of money in hand is more worthwhile than a steadfast kindness of heart. The principle of evil is the devil sometimes, and sometimes it is many small devils. Then again, it is the vicious temper or the false idea. The whole claim might just as well be met by us now and faced up with the question. How much profit is there in it? How much power? How much satisfaction? Jesus

Christ called the whole claim nothing. "A lie," He said. There is nothing to the whole of it.

The high church dignitaries were greatly afraid that the young man who made such stupendous affirmation of Himself and the fishermen would upset everything. And so He would. They would soon find out that there was a greater among them, and no lesser. They would soon find out that there were no Romans, and no Jews, no high priests and no lepers.

All these were a lie of belief in a partial God. There is in reality no such being. A menial task like washing the feet is no lower than the blowing of Gabriel's trumpets *"There is one Lord (Law) and His name One."*

Jesus preached this boldly and lived it just as boldly. He ate with publicans and sinners. He touched the lepers. He blessed sick women. He washed men's feet. Having proclaimed the principle that all are one He must act it out.

He told the commonest kind of mixed audiences to have the faith of God. How could they have the faith of God? In order to have a faith equal to God's faith they must certainly have the courage to affirm omnipresence, omnipotence, omniscience.

Somewhere there was a teaching then, dropping around into whatever soil would receive it, to the effect that the mind is as great as it has courage to affirm and demonstrates its greatness to the extent it has confidence in its affirmations.

Knowing this truth, you see, Jesus could not ask them to affirm any less of themselves than He knew they had a right to. He was not perceiving their flesh. He was not examining their intellect. He was recognizing their divinity.

Napoleon walked over the French generals by affirming his power to do so and handled them like chessmen because he had the self-conviction he could do it.

How high have you affirmed of yourself. How much courage in affirmation have you sprung to?

You have the teachings of Jesus to the effect that there is no substance to you except Spirit. And Spirit is God. Whatever you give voice to you may be sure you will expand to its stature. Would you not like to forget all things except your omnipotence, omniscience, omnipresence? Then do forget all things in the affirmations of your spirit.

Now there is a law of the effect of a truth told which makes it seem as if you had to face up evil appearances after you have spoken very highly of yourself with your mind. Grief, anger, disappointment, failure appear just like these natural consequences of Jesus and Judas and the high priests meeting with such different affirmations. You must make a firm soil of character by a declaration of faith, after which the most servile duties will be ennobled by your doing them.

In the midst of your anger, or grief or disappointment utter this idea intensely; "I do believe that my God is now working with me, through me and by me and for me, to make me omnipresent, omnipotent, omniscient."

Directly your mind will take a new base. The experience will be exactly like the precipitating of camphor when water is dropped into the alcohol holding it in solution. Your mind now fixes its faith. After your faith is grounded your words will bring to pass wonderfully.

You remember Jesus Christ did not say, according to your denials, or according to you affirmations, but according to your faith.

Here at this point of the knowledge of His greatness, the faith in His greatness, He was as meek as a slave of the Orient, faithful as a mother to her baby; He washed their feet. The greater the sweep of His affirmation, the lower His condescension of love.

You often see that in great and able men there is less ostentation than in those pretending to be great and not believing in their greatness. Von Moltke attended a peasant baby like a good brother while its sister who had it in charge went to see the king and the great General pass by. When she was disappointed at not seeing Von Moltke in the crowd he invited her to the hotel, where he appeared in full uniform.

A small officer would not have done it unless he had believed in his own greatness of spirit. Then if the small officer had so believed in greatness of spirit he would soon be taking the honors of Moltke. It is such a glorious knowledge to enter into: that we are as great as we have courage to expand into (or affirm of ourselves) and can demonstrate as much greatness as we believe in.

He who taught us of our inheritance of power, our kingly heirship, taught us meekness and docility. Fidelity to any task is the exhibition of God. The understanding of Peter needed washing or clarifying. His pledge to the ministry was already being well carried out (hands) so Jesus did not wash his hands and head. Once he recognized the Messiah he had not to recognize Him over again, but only to understand His teachings.

Here are the cleansing waters for your understanding; "In my good there is no mixture of evil. On my spirit there is no burden. There is no absence of life, substance, or intelligence." There is nothing to hate. "There is no sin, sickness, death in my idea of good."

Now you may make the highest affirmation your courage will spring to. You are already it. Have faith in yourself. Do the loyal service of true greatness.

Right in that lot where you are called to serve is the chance to exercise your talent. What lies nearest at hand, do bravely. An artist may be sending the glory of living pictures into the imagination of some bed-bound child while she tends the baking in her country home.

No genius is lost to the world because its fame is not yet emblazoned. The high preparation time is thinking your highest while doing lowest tasks. Tasks, which require no thought, give time for the noblest thoughts. See how the doctrine of this Servant of men comes quickening our hopes today. As great as you have courage to mentally proclaim yourself and sure to demonstrate as well as your faith in your greatness, decides! Therefore have faith in God. Have the faith of God. There is no self-sacrifice, "I am myself now and I know myself. My highest idea: I am it!"

"So is every heart that knows the right,

And choosing it, rejoices

That what it thinks is true,

Itself is that."

October 18, 1891

LESSON IV

POWER OF THE MIND

John 14:13; 15-27

Jesus Christ said to His people when He was about to go away out of their sight and they were deeply troubled about it, *"Let not your heart be troubled. . . I go to prepare a place for you . . . The Comforter whom the Father will send in My Name shall teach you all things."*

His command at this particular time to these disturbed hearts is evidence of His knowledge of the supreme power of mind over the most intense feelings. He evidently did not believe in letting the passions master mankind, even though the recognized leaders of thought were teaching the world at that time that since the passions are masters of mankind and not mankind of the passions there is no way of ridding ourselves of the passions but by annihilation.

Look at the man torn by jealousy; who is the master, himself or jealousy? Look at him under the wind of anger; who is master, the man or anger? To live thinking this is not life, therefore let us be rid of life. But Jesus of Nazareth paid no attention to sophistries. He knew that every man is as great as he has courage to declare himself and will demonstrate as much greatness as he has confidence in his affirmations. "I am myself now that I know myself. My highest ideal — I am it! So is every heart that knows the right, and choosing it, rejoices that what it thinks is true — itself is that."

He had already taught them of their equality with Himself, and here again He reiterates that He and His Father are in them and that if He goes out of their sight and mind as a man of flesh and blood they will be so thrown upon their own indwelling spirit that they will better realize their power and greatness. He did not believe in greater and lesser. He believed in universal equality through universal recognition of the truth concerning the impartial God indwelling everywhere.

There is nothing more heart-breaking than separation from those you love best. There is nothing more despair-filling and frenzy-stirring than to see the failure of all your cherished plans, your earthly hopes and ambitions, with abundant evidence that even your religious aspirations will never be realized, and nothing of your teaching will demonstrate what you have proclaimed. This was the state of mind of those men the Master was talking to.

Those Jews, who had given up their old form of faith for the one He taught, and had publicly espoused Him and His cause, were now told that He was to be crucified as a malefactor in the utmost disgrace. They were told that He would leave them to the companionship of a being or principle of action, which they had never seen, viz., the Holy Ghost. Their hopes had been raised to the highest pitch of enthusiasm that their Messiah would conquer the Romans and set Israel free. They hoped for the noblest prosperity of His teachings. His triumph would be their triumph. They wanted to see the old church converted to their Teacher's doctrine of the unreality of material things and the reality of Spirit. They hoped to see their Master's announcement that the devil is a lie from the beginning prevail — not so much because it was true, but to triumph over the rest.

They were sure in some mysterious way that all things seen and touched are but symbols of what is real, and as their chosen leader was making great demonstrations in explanation of how the wonderful healings were performed by the miracle workers of all ages, they wanted to see Him succeed.

He made God seem so real to them, so near, so mighty to save, so substantial, yet evidently they loved the man Jesus better than they did the God He preached. There had been a great many strong minds teaching that ideas are the only real things, but at present Jesus was more comforting than an idea of one.

Their love for Him was intense. Their reverence for Him was unbounded. Their confidence in His power was stupendous. So their disappointment at the way things were turning out had troubled their hearts with anguish. It was the opportunity of Jesus to give them the best lesson in self-treatment that He had ever given. It is very good to know how to treat ourselves so as to be in no need of a physician. It is better to understand self-cure than to rely upon the best doctor in creation. The effect of disappointment and grief is disease, waste of property and finally death. Socrates had taught this law long before Jesus Christ. So right here was the chance to handle the cause of poverty and disease before it had resulted in anything — while it was raging.

Political disappointments, social humiliation, religious despair: He told them not to let these feelings have any place in their being. He said He had their highest good at heart, and unless He went away they would never step forward into their rightful place at all. They must know that it was totally unscientific to lean upon any man, woman, or child for strength, power or advancement. He personified all their thought of leaning — all their inclination to depend upon something or somebody, and not until they put Him out of their mind as a personal being would their mind spring forward into its rightful place.

They had stood back and let Him in person, not principle, fill all their mind, till He was their support, their teacher, their defender, and the principle He taught was lost sight of. They literally must step forward in their own estimation as Spirit. They were in substance self-increasing and self-supporting, self-defending and self-rewarding. "My mind to me a kingdom is."

It is better to love principle than persons. If we love principle best we find ourselves growing in strength, or, rather, showing forth that strength which we always had. We find ourselves showing forth better and better judgment. We find ourselves more and more the personifications of fearlessness. If we love persons best we find ourselves swayed more or less, swerved more or less from our highest judgments.

Such is the effect of dependence upon people for our happiness, or support, that, even while we are not with them, the thoughts they are thinking cause our fears and tremblings, our elations, and depressions, which seem so unaccountable. There is no dependence to be placed upon one who is good because his love for or his fear of his companions make him so. When a stronger love or a stronger fear stirs him he will go its way. Your child kept from tobacco simply because he is afraid of you or loves you is not safe. There is a way of teaching that will make the love of right in the heart, and all the tobacco stores and saloons in a great city would be no temptation.

It is better to learn this teaching than to deal with people. There is a way of thinking in the secrecy of your own room that will cause the shadows of temptation to fall away as nothingness. The Word of this principle is omnipotent. Temptations flee. Appetites fall. Anger is forgotten. It is the Word of Truth concerning the Spirit of mankind; the responsive, noble Spirit, indwelling everywhere. "If I make my bed in hell (send my word down to the worst seeming of evil) Thou, God, art there."

> *"Sharper than steel is the sword of the Spirit,*
>
> *Swifter than arrows the word of the Truth is,*
>
> *Stronger than anger is love and subdueth."*

This does not mean that you are not to love your friends and your family. By no means. But it does mean that your love is a sentimental feeling, not capable of withstanding the pressure of some temptation peculiarly powerful over you, till you are grounded into principle first.

"Principle is God. Seek first the kingdom of God and all these things (friends unfailing, goods abiding) will be added." To Jesus, religious supremacy, political victory, social honors, counted for nothing, except they were the out-showing of a true principle proclaimed and lived. He knew that a church that is held together and owns its memberships by reason of the personal influence of a man is on a shaky foundation. A government that trusts its name and honor to one whose name and honor are not synonyms of a mighty principle is laying a foundation of quicksand.

God is awake — alive. There is no social prestige, attainable worth noticing if it is secured by your personal magnetism, your natural possessions, your education, if you do not stand to your companions as the exponent of some worthy cause which is the principle you live.

When a great preacher is careless about his many obligations, or keeping his engagements, and as a respecter of persons, there is a screw loose in the future prospects of the church. They saw in Jesus the man their ambitions fulfilled. They must see in the principle He preached the glory of the world.

"Ah, but," you say, "you would not have us entrust a ship in a storm to a man simply because he was good when the captain who is recognized as a bad man understands sailing? You would not trust the government to a good man when the bad man is the better statesman? The ship is not safe if the captain is not upright, and the government will court downfall from its deliberate choice of an immoral statesman. What do you think of that time when the fair ship on smooth waters was sailing so peacefully under its notedly good captain, and a lover of God suddenly came to him in the night and urged him to steer the ship straight north? The captain laughed at him but upon his appearing three times during the night with the same entreaty, finally did turn the ship, and was saved from the iceberg floating down from the north, preparing to meet the ship at right angles.

What do you think of the ship in the hurricane with her greatly trusted captain and trained crew utterly hopeless, when the man who dwelt in the midst of the principle of righteousness said, "Turn this way," and at once they were swung into that center of peace which is the heart of the cyclone, the hurricane, the simoon, the whirling suns?

This principle of goodness trusted, regardless of external fitness, is the government which shall "reign from sea to sea and from the river to the uttermost parts of the earth."

"Of its kingdom there shall be no end." Under its reign no mother will die, no child meet with accident. Love and trust this principle and all things that you can ask, better than you can imagine, will

"Rise from the deeps,

Sail over the seas

And down from the stars

Haste, the nations to please."

Jesus had taught these people this law of trust in the right: trust in the good itself. But no, they crowded their human relations, Himself included, into their heart so tightly that they were even then losing sight of the principles He announced. They quarreled as to who should be the greatest in the kingdom of heaven — greatest in the Spirit!

They forbade children, women, beggars, to get near their majestic leader. But He said all were equal in God, He spoke of the sure goodness of children. He called the despised women daughters of God; He asked the beggars tenderly what service He could render them, touching the lepers as though they were princes.

He trusted to the principle He proclaimed to hold its own. He preached eternal life and trusted the principle itself to take Him safely through. He trusted to goodness itself to feed and house and clothe Him, and laid Himself so hard to the winds of His teaching that it did feed, clothe, house Him.

Hero worship is not good. It is that for which the heroes stand that we worship, then our love for them is healthy. He knew that the noble thoughts and trust in God of ages of goodness bloomed in Him. Did not the poetic feelings and unconscious observations of the past of Anglo-Saxon human experiences find expression in Shakespeare? So Jesus Christ was the bloom into manifest life of the confidence of all who had lived before Him, that goodness is safer to trust than human skill. Elisha's confidence in his God as able to do mighty works had turned away from the gates of Samaria the armed besiegers, when the King and his lords had failed. Worldly policy had starved the people, but trust in God put fine wheat and sweet barley into their fingers.

Where did the wars and the famines and the pestilences (worldly policies carried out) spring from? But Jesus was the fruit of trust in God. His teachings would save from all evil. To watch flesh or material processes is deteriorating. To say that Spirit is the only substance, we do not believe in any law but the Spirit, is increasing in health, increasing in judgment, increasing in prosperity.

Shall we not hear this Man teach that even to look at Himself as a Man is to forget principle, and either get to hating or loving without judgment?

Dante was looked at as a person trying to put his fame up, and they ignored his principle and exiled him; Socrates likewise; Columbus the same; also Bruno, Galileo.

Cleopatra was personally adored, and her people were slain at her whim, smiling at her with love. But principle studied, loved, obeyed, puts us into our right mind — the place prepared for us. There is room enough in omnipresence for us to spread the wings of our love over all the earth. There is power enough in omnipotence for our spirit to conquer the elements. Principle studied increases us to be one with it. So Christ comes again as doctrine, principle, spirit, and makes His abode in us as God, and then there is no taking away of our joy.

There is no oneness with Christ until we understand His teachings. The love of the personal Man is not what He taught. He took that away for the principle of righteousness to be first in our mind. He lives and reigns as an eternal teaching concerning the dominion of goodness. There is nothing to expect from human statesmanship, religious supremacies, social elevations. All things to expect from putting all these things out of mind to understand the principle of righteousness, as to its power, its efficiency, its swift-coming to conquer. This comforts. And the Comforter is the Holy Ghost.

October 25, 1891

LESSON V

VINES AND BRANCHES

John 15:1-16

It is the nature of vines to put forth branches. It is the nature of mind to put forth thoughts. Every thought of the mind bears fruit after its kind. The mind of Jesus Christ thought only pure thoughts, so all His works were perfect. Every thought the mind thinks personifies in some circumstance, or thing, or human being before our eyes. No two people see the circumstance, or object, or person exactly the same. Each mind sees its own belief about the matter. When we all believe the truth we shall all see everything exactly as it is, John, James, Matthew, Philip, Peter, etc., all stood for true ideas in the mind of Jesus.

John represented His tenderness. James personified His strong word that He so often spoke to others. Matthew stood for His benevolent thought; he never failed to speak when a case could be best reached by being benevolent toward it instead of strong, or tender, or argumentative. "Find out men's wants and will and meet them there."

Philip was His swift word. Some of our thoughts go instantaneously where we are thinking. See how quickly Philip ran towards the eunuch in the chariot of the Queen of Ethiopia and converted him in no time. Peter stood for the idea that people want substantial help like bread and meat and health and shelter, rather than promises of comfort in a future paradise. All these ideas are good ones and Jesus Christ said that was because His mind was so true. "I am the true vine." "My Father is the husbandman." My good judgment keeps me from thinking anything but truth. Husbandman always means good judgment. There is only one side of the question when good judgment handles your vine (that is, your mind and its thoughts).

There is no power given to evil at all. All thoughts of feebleness or weakness or inefficiency are lopped off and burned up. You have nothing to do with them. Did you ever have a good, kind feeling towards anybody, and when you saw them sick or crying you pitifully wished you could do something for them, but felt powerless to do what they needed? If you had understood this lesson well you would not have felt powerless, you would have known that your kindly feeling towards them contained within itself the ability to draw from the very forces of the universe all the help they needed to them.

That kindly feeling put into a definite word whether silent or audible should be pruned of the useless twig of helpless feeling. Euripides said, "One right thought is worth a hundred right hands." So it is. The thought that backs the action is what wins.

Abraham Lincoln spent a whole night putting forth his loving kindness of heart over the universe to bring help to what he considered a righteous cause.

And the principle of loving kindness in the universe stirred as waters stir when we throw a stone into them, and the loving kindness in every heart was stirred, aware or unaware of what moved it to respond, "we're coming!"

The captain of the Monitor hastened, he knew not why, the unpromising boat stirred as though it were alive, and the crews fired the airs to victory. He would not take no for an answer. He would not receive any other action from the universe but loving kindness. Loving kindness in the heart put forth into the airs of loving kindness will wake the echoes again and again till everything that can help your neighbor comes hurrying to help him. There is plenty to help him with. Get it. You get it if your refuse to feel helpless. Does not the vine that is pruned draw rich sustenance? Mind is all. It will turn the hands and train the voice and trim the actions to success. A man on a desert island cast away with the rest of the crew of a ship took the thought, "Living Water," into his mind instead of describing how thirsty he was. It was very hot and they were dying of thirst, but while the rest were putting the forces of their minds into describing their thirst, their heat, their misery, he put the whole force of his mind into the words, "Living Water, Living Water!"

These words caused his hands to seize a spade or shovel, and these words caused him to begin to dig, while his companions' words caused them to lie down in despair on the hot sand.

They derided him, but he did not notice. The words of his mind mastered everything. So did theirs. But you see his words were very different from theirs, even under the same circumstances. "By thy words thou art justified." Michelangelo never noticed how rough or how hard the marble was — he was thinking of the image. This man struck the Living Water and it was so deep that they had to help him out or he would have been drowned they said.

You must trust the loving kindness of your heart. Can you not say, "Loving Kindness, in you is sufficient help?"

You do not remember you have no money, no influence, that people have thought you too sympathetic; all you think of is the omnipotence of loving kindness. This is a possible state of mind. When a child or companion seems to get into wrong ways why do you droop and cry when you know that there really is a little struggling hope in your heart that he will do better some time?

That very hope is the salvation of the loved one. Refuse every thought but your hope. Let all the force of your mind rally to trust your hope. Hope, even so little a streak of it, is better than ten thousand men at work to help you. Hope is the best beloved messenger of God. She was never yet killed. Men and women have shut down on her, tried to smother her, hid her deep in their bosoms, but immortal defender that she is, she was never quenched yet.

Trust your hope. Never mind who tells you the particulars of downfall or disaster — trust your hope. It is a branch from the deathless soul that dwells in you as the true vine or true creation of God.

"I trust Thee, Hope!" Run all your energy into your confidence in your hope to lead you to success. "But it would have to be a miracle," you say, "to bring this state of affairs out to my satisfaction, for the situation is irretrievable, according to human judgment."

Who cares anything for human judgment? It is God's judgment that tells a Michelangelo there is a goddess, or a David, or an angel in the rough marble, and tells a man on the island that there is Living Water -where none was ever found before! There is not time or energy to be spent in crying. Lean hard to the winds of your hope. Your highest aspiration is that which you are intended to fulfill, and if you have heretofore let any environments or circumstances sap your confidence in your aspirations, it is time you pruned your ideas.

Here Jesus Christ assures them that let His words abide in them; they may ask what they will and it will be done. The student of astronomy would know more about the stars after an hour of trust in his hope to know, than after years of patient investigation of the heavens. Once an astronomer searching the skies in vain and figuring in vain, told one who knew nothing about stars his dilemma. The other was a firm truster in the law that "the Spirit will teach you all things." He responded quickly, an answer, which the astronomer proved to be accurate.

Miracles are your birthright. That is what your hope tells you and your hope is correct.

You shall see every man, woman and child saved if your goodness of heart will receive all your living forces. Here is a book written by a man who scans material stars and reckons on the letter of prophecy, and he says that we are on the verge of destruction as an unbelieving race. We live in the last week of history. The "Holy Spirit grieved beyond all endurance" is about to leave us to face incarnate evil.

Now what does the husbandman of your mind — its good judgment, say of a Holy Spirit that gives up the fight so easily as that, when the prize to be won is the redemption of a race whose only crime is that they have listened to a teaching just like his, viz, that they must smother hope?

No. The sorrowful planet shall sing for joy and "the gates of hell shall not prevail against" the Truth. The worst of mankind is as entitled to the best of the universe as the best of us, for the worst of them have not refused to trust their hope (the one branch that puts forth from the soul again and again, even to the last breath of consciousness) any more than the best of us. "Herein is my Father glorified that ye bear much fruit." Not any little scrimpling achievements, but the safety of a globe is your mission. Did you ever trust a friend that what he told you of truth was true?

Listen. What hope tells you of truth is true. Trust her and you trust God, for she is the truth of God. Faith in her will quicken and quicken faith till the universe only shall be large enough to contain your faith.

Do you look longingly for mankind to be just — for goodness to prevail? That longing is the stir of the goodness in your heart. Trust that stir. She is hope unfurling her white wings. Assure her that you trust her. I trust thee. Hope! Come, goodness, come! "The nations shall learn war no more."

"The wicked cease." Hope has been rewarded with all she ever asked of mankind, namely confidence in her. Over there in the business mart whither your trembling footsteps go tomorrow, fearing there may be disaster waiting, stirs one little hope that a miracle may be wrought to save you? Tell that little hope you love it. Tell it you trust it. It speaks to the Principle of Bounty —

God omnipotent, omniscient!" Hope has been more faithful to God than any messenger to man. Give her your trust, and she will work any miracle you ask. "Ye shall ask what you will." "Have hope towards God." "It shall be done unto you."

"Bright drink the angels

From her glory,

Though none have scanned

Her glorious way!

Bright speak the words of

Her living story,

And over our star

Dawns her endless day!"

"Henceforth I call you not servants but friends ... for all things that I have heard from the Father I have told you." Now Jesus Christ is in them when they know all the words that He knows and they speak all that He speaks and they trust their words as He trusts.

The Comforter is that power that comes into your consciousness with the name Jesus Christ. That name is the saving Truth. You had better speak it until the same mind fills and thrills you that thrilled the only One who ever demonstrated supreme mastery over all kinds of claims of evil. "In My Name the devils tremble. In my Name the power of the Holy Spirit reigns triumphant. In My Name immortal life. In My Name goodness. I am the true vine. The way I begin to reign in you is when you trust your highest aspirations, your only hope, and prune boldly the tremblings of apprehension, of short-sightedness of prophecies of evil. Nothing shall prevail against Me," says Jesus Christ, in man the hope of glory.

November 1, 1891

LESSON VI

YOUR IDEA OF GOD

John 16:1-15

The swift summary of text for our notice is Jesus Christ's prophecy: *"Whosoever killeth you will think that he doeth God service, because they have not known the Father nor Me, It is expedient for you that I go away; for if I go not away the Comforter will not come. He will reprove the world and guide you into all truth."*

When one is speaking of nature or the nature of man he either means the carnal nature, with its blind force, whose operations bring earthquakes and cyclones, bloodshed and bondages, or he means that deep sense of righteousness implanted in every creature which John called *"the Light that lighteth every man."*

Two people speaking of the nature of man will greatly differ, and one will grossly misunderstand the other simply because the other is speaking from the standpoint of the spiritual nature while

49

he is making conclusions from physical experiences. One says it is the nature of man to think thoughts whose outcome will be corporations and whose intentions shall be to make your daily bread impossible and your meat a thing of memory.

They insist that it is nature's exercise of itself in men which make them unjust toward women. It is natural, they tell us, to connive against the weaker when the stronger is pitted against it. Man is but following out his inherent nature when he makes sex distinctions, and laughs in his sleeve at the deserted wife, the hungry bird, the drowning baby, for does not nature's sun shine and her rivers run smiling on, indifferent to the welfare of men or angels?

"Sweet and low the west winds blow,

Careless sing as they careless know.

How hearts were broken long ago."

Nature connives against the helpless, against women, against minorities. "Therefore says the English Lionel Beale, what is wanted is something to upset natural law."

It is well he puts into conscious expression the unconscious wish of the world. It is the stir of the bird's wing for the air it was made to fly in, for truly they who would choose to see every creature on the planet glad and protected and powerful, stand ready to put their hand on the main spring of sorrow and say "Broken!" and their fingers to the clock of time of pain and say "Stop!" so soon as they shall know this law, so plainly taught in this lesson by Jesus. "He shall reprove the world and send the Comforter."

Another says, "There is no such nature to stop. The only nature there is that is real is the principle of righteousness stirring within all men and all creatures. The savages know what it is right to do. The hordes in the slums of London choose that the brave young men and the good young girl in the play shall come off victorious when trickery is pitted against them, else they will hiss the play." "This is nature," says one whose face is set that way till he sees nothing else. Pythagoras called it the salt of men in all ages. Plutarch called it the unerring guide; Socrates called it the Divine sign; John said it lighted every man that ever came into the world.

So One Man, determined to let this nature speak its own way with all its might, through Him, said in triumph, "All power is given unto Me in heaven and in earth." Then the rest seized upon Him because He, being a man like themselves, made Himself God. He carefully taught them, the mortal shall not say, I am God. Only the immortal shall speak of its Godhood. But, looking at the flesh as the truth of themselves, they fought against the speech of the Spirit. The flesh warreth against the Spirit to this day when you two are speaking together. One of you insists that God does not send the cyclone and earthquake, the famine and the survival of the stronger. The other says; "He must, because He made all things, and surely we see that these things exist."

One of you says, "There is but one side of this question, viz., the God side," The other says, "There is the side of the law which sends evil as good." These disciples of Jesus were here being prepared to speak only from the standpoint of the Spirit of Good, when in aftertime men assail them with the claim of the power of evil. They could not speak entirely from that standpoint while a Man with infinite powers to protect and feed them stood near them, upon whom they might lean.

He showed how by speaking and thinking entirely from the standpoint of the principle of right He could increase loaves and fishes and gold at their call. He did what the whole body of Jews did not dare to do with the moneychangers who, having got hold of all the Hebrew coins, made the people pay heavy premiums for half-shekel pieces. He put them out bodily and made them respect Him as a force He could demonstrate when He pleased. His disciples forgot the principle He announced in their admiration of its feats. So He went away to throw them on their own understanding of Truth. They were beset by those who verily thought they were doing their God service by opposing them.

And truly if it was the God they believed in who ruled the world, they were right pleasing unto Him, for the god of the external world as described by those who see it, is glad when a Lisbon lies low and a Johnstown swims in tears.

But the true God is mercy, tenderness, and loving kindness. This is the God of Jesus Christ.

"God is love. His mercy brightens

All the path in which we rove.

Bliss He wakes, and woe He lightens,

God is wisdom, God is love."

In Jonah's time "every man prayed unto his God." It makes all the difference in the creation to your powers and experiences what God you believe in and what you believe your God does.

Elijah had supposed God sent the cyclone and earthquake and famine, but being a sincere man his heart was in ashes of despair, just as every heart is that is mistaken in its suppositions about God; so he became silent, and found that the still small Voice counseling mercy and tenderness and freedom was the true God Thus he had not been true to the true God in slaying the prophets of Baal at the brook Kishon

Thus supposition about God, and not God indeed, had stirred to earthquakes and hot winds of terror. The Roman governors and pro-consuls afterward hunted the Christians to please their imaginary God, viz., the sender of calamities. They tied them to wild beasts and set them for bonfires in Nero's gardens.

But,

> *"Speak, Victory! Who are life's victors?*
>
> *Unroll thy long annals and say!*
>
> *Are they those whom the world called the victors,*
>
> *Who won the success of a day?*
>
> *The Spartans who fell at Thermopylae's tryst,*
>
> *Or the Persians and Xerxes?*
>
> *The martyrs or Nero?*
>
> *Pilate or Christ?"*

I am my own idea of God. Nothing can be plainer than that I am my own idea of God, and you are your own idea of God.

The man who chases from the prize fight to the gambling hall believes in a God who chases him around seeing every evil thing he does and getting a punishment ready while he himself has things just as he pleases regardless of the feelings of others. Those who believe nearest in the true God are safest. Those whose idea of God is absolutely true are absolutely safe.

What God do you believe in? What is your idea of God? John Knox had been thinking what a mighty fortress is our God when he found himself rising from his place at the table. A bullet came crashing through the window, but he was safe. Mungo Park thought of his God as his unfailing provider. But he forgot to think so at one time and was utterly destitute in the wilds of Africa. A little cheery tuft of live moss reminded him of its happy trust of his own God and as soon as he took hold of the true God again he was amply provided with all things. "Do you think asked a pious believer in the God who sends earthquakes and famines, "that you can make an impression on 4,000,000 Chinese?" "No," said the Doctor, "but my God can." This God was different from the God of Louis XIV, for he compelled the Huguenots at the point of the bayonet by fire to destroy 700 churches because they did not worship as he did.

Richard Boyle, Earl of Cork, rose from the lowest position to the highest rank by taking for his motto, "God's good providence is my inheritance." A child living with a mother who had an idea that God sends poverty and want took it into his mind that God would hear every time they scraped the bottom of the meal barrel. And the child's idea fed them.

I am my own idea of God. It was a step ahead for the child to have an idea of God that He would not let them actually starve, but it is a greater step to have the true idea, viz., that God never lets His children have any bottom to their barrels of plenty. If the idea of Good is the mainspring of human experience, you have the power to upset the apparent order of things.

If your idea of God swings the clock to the time of pain and poverty you may stop it when you please. Jesus Christ told you to keep that affirmation of His till you should strike down the idea of God that throttles the nations.

"All power is given unto Me."

Jesus Christ had the true idea of God. God is Love. John said: "If a man love God he will love his brother also." Whatever your idea of God is what you will treat your family with. A mother who had an idea that God sends sickness for some good purpose blew the simoon of this notion against her little girl and she had typhoid fever. Then she besought that God of hers to remove the fever that her own idea was plowing like a hot wind over the child. All to no purpose. Because she had an idea that God sometimes does and sometimes does not do as you want Him to. By and by she went into a room, alone and took off her thought from the little girl and put up her thought entirely to the true God that His good will might be done and that she should see that good will.

Then the child got well at once. The true God always wills well. Never anything else. Look out there at the mainspring of your world what you are doing! Do not let it be said of you as of Nero and that mother, "because they have not known the Father nor me."

Physicians sit in judgment on a man. They believe in nature's laws of waste and decay and death. *"According to thy faith be it unto thee."* So they blow their cold idea over the man. Yet when they should look away from him they would say that one with the true idea of God could restore him to health. While they are looking away he breathes better. Why do they not spend all their time and all their energies studying that law of the true idea of God that can always heal as Jesus healed? That idea that fills the mind touches other minds. Keeley the motor man has thought of force, we are told, till he can start a whole swing of machinery to working which the best mechanic cannot stir till Keeley touches him on the shoulder. When the true idea of God fills the mind you shall touch shoulder to shoulder with all the universe of mankind till health and joy and peace reign supreme.

You must withdraw your ideas of mankind being subject to natural laws of fire and frost, death and sickness. The true idea of God gives you the true idea of mankind. They shall feel your touch on the mainspring of the universe. If the child of his generation can stir the machinery of the factories by his idea of force you shall stir the nations by your idea of God.

Jesus Christ promised all things to them that should hold His Name in mind. His Name should forever stand for the true idea of God. The Comforter should come in His Name. The world should be reproved. Those who have held His Name in mind till it has gone away as man and has come in as the principle of righteousness, have seen those they meet change from foolish-appearing to wise; from unsteady to reliable. "Who so findeth Me findeth life." "In Me shall all the nations of the earth be blessed." When we strike at the false idea of God and let the true idea live we are letting Jesus Christ live as He meant in us: not as flesh but as Truth. "And Christ lives on in His strength and glory. He lives and loves with a love divine. By the light of His Name I read life's story. And the key to the world is mine."

November 8th, 1891

LESSON VII

MAGIC OF HIS NAME

John 17:1-19

Jesus teaches all about prayer in this lesson. He discloses His mission to the world, the mission of His disciples and your mission also.

Here He sets apart certain ones to devote all their time, energy, money, mind, life, to preaching the truth concerning the true God. Henceforth they should not be known among men as lawyers and physicians or fishermen, but as preachers of the peculiar doctrine of Jesus Christ. Here, you observe for the first time, He calls the Name in which all the miracles of the future are to be wrought — Jesus Christ.

He had told them of the magic power of His Name. In it was contained the power of the Holy Ghost to comfort, heal, rejoice, prosper. By thinking His Name they were to be imbued with power from on high, and illuminated with great spiritual understanding.

It was customary in old times for miracles to be wrought by speaking certain names. They spoke these names inaudibly. They would not tell the name they used in some cases because the careless use of the name would not accomplish anything. Each name stood for certain powers and limitations of powers. It represented much. The Egyptians used Serapis, Osiris, Isis. The Indians used Buddha. The Persians used Ormuzd. Brainerd, the missionary to our American Indians, could not tempt them by the name Jesus Christ, because they had names that were miracle working.

Constantine noticed that the names used by the heathen worked destruction more than life. He tested one of his magicians on a fierce bull. When the magician whispered one name into its ear the animal fell dead. The same name whispered into the dead ear would not raise the beast to life. But a Christian, who had supreme faith in the name Jesus Christ, raised the animal to life instantly with that Name.

All those old practices which we have so long regarded as worthless superstitions, we are now finding out to be hints of the way to our own demonstrations of power and goodness. He had told them to put out of their horizon their father, mother, husband, wife, children, that His Name might start the wheels of their mind and life over again. Did you ever try holding His Name in mind to the exclusion of all other names till its high significance as salvation from all evil came thrilling and quickening you with delight?

No? Then how can you judge as to whether He was mistaken when telling the world that all its prayers should be granted in His Name?

You would like to heal all the sickness of the world, ease all its misery, rejoice all its hearts. You have tried many ways. Have you tried that Name till its significance as the demonstration of God through you worked miracles? If you are eager to help the world — so eager that you would do anything, as you have so often said — try writing this Name in every blood-drop and on every string of your heart.

He said you would be found preaching the good word without any mixture of evil. (The idea of evil is the son of perdition. He taught that every son or word of His mind would demonstrate except the word of perishing, or devil word, the lie-from-the-beginning word. The errors should not count.) You are to heal, stop vicious tempers, raise all who seem to be dead to life again. Then if you faithfully work at these things with His Name in mind you need not take any thought about what to eat, drink, wear, nor as to whom you shall marry nor - what you shall lay up for old age. The four works will make the living on the square which will then draw around you the perfect circle of a beautiful and satisfied life.

And if you can demonstrate satisfactory living, you can teach others how to demonstrate. You must not only be sanctified yourself, but all the world must be as glad as yourself. "He lifted up His eyes." This is stated not carelessly. The way the mind thinks will teach the way the eyes turn. Take the man who is always meditating on high themes for his own sake, and he will look down. The man who thinks with his head down is apt to conclude to do things to advantage himself whether others are advantaged or not. The man who looks straight ahead is one who gets on fairly well with the world and generally gets to feeling that he can hold his own with the world. He often gets philanthropic and wide-hearted. The man whose thoughts are on God as all, has an upward look of eyes that, without being conspicuous, you catch while you converse with him. The man who brings all his help from above and acknowledges it, does not believe anything is impossible. The man who looks out straight towards the horizons, believes in great obstacles and names what he must meet. The man who looks down believes in submission to the existing order of things and feels that he must yield to the worst with as good a face as he can make up.

The Chinese teach certain kinds of people to sit in a circle and practice steadily looking up to a clear stone that will drop down, sometimes answers to their needs. A colored washerwoman had got the idea into her mind that "de good Lawd was a showerin' blessin's on" her from His seat in heaven.

A nice pious woman told her with the corners of her sad mouth downcast like her eyes, that it seemed dreadful to her to see so much levity and lightness where there was so much likelihood of misery to come any day, "Supposing you are taken sick with rheumatism and can't work; or supposing your employer dies?" she was arguing.

"Stop!" said the washerwoman, "I neber suppose nuffm. De 'Lawd is my Shepherd 'n I shall not want,' and, Honey, it is yo'r supposin' as is makin'yo' so mis'able."

Jesus Christ had just been looking around on them all. "I call you not servants, but friends." Then He took them as one with Him to the Holy High Place, where all His thoughts dwelt in exalted ecstasy and called down the healing glory of the God within Him. All who have tried mental healing have found that an exalted state of mind or an ecstatic state of mind where the glory of God is seen and realized as very near and real is a sure healing state. Then it is found that it is very direct communion with this down-falling glory to praise and bless and glorify It. To thank It. To give all credit to It. Cromwell asked the House of Commons to give God the whole glory of his victory at Naseby. Jesus Christ was praising God for the crucifixion, as to its outcome. He did not see the crucifixion: He saw the time when we should know Him as principle demonstrated, not as a man of flesh and blood. Whoever undertakes to be spiritually minded or to look straight to God for all things, will always come out successful.

The business man seeing God will find that when every bit of news brought to him is bad, every deal he makes slips up, his collectors run away with rents, etc., that at the end he has had more income than if all these had come out right when he was not seeing God nigh within the exalted place of his mind. Nor height nor depth nor any other creature can keep you from demonstrating success when you glorify God for His Being. Of course God is not in the ether of the sky. God is in His kingdom within your mind. The eyes just signal or symbolize your way of thinking.

Chrysostom was threatened with exile if he preached God in Christ Jesus.

> *"Thou canst not exile me. The world is my Father's house."*
>
> *"I will slay thee."*
>
> *"Thou canst not. God is my life,"*
>
> *"I will take away thy possessions."*
>
> *"Thou canst not. They are in God."*
>
> *"I will take away thy friends."*
>
> *"Thou canst not. God is my friend."*

A missionary in Russia was once waited on by a court official to tell him that his Imperial Sovereign would not consent to his preaching Christ Jesus in that kingdom. The missionary said, "My

Imperial Sovereign does not ask anybody's consent to send His good word through His own Kingdom."

There is nothing can withstand your power of influence when you give God the glory of your life, your health, your possessions. Queen Mary feared John Knox more than she did an army of ten thousand soldiers. All good is from God. "I drew them with the bands of love, and they knew not that I healed them. Let us praise God who dwelleth in the high place of our own mind. Praise God for healing us before we see the healing." "I healed them and they knew it not."

Your bodily organs love to be praised. A thousand little mouths are stretching open within you, hungry for praising. You must praise your heart for its sweet happy beating.

Do you not know that its substance is God? Praise your liver for its lovely life and wholesome working. Its action is God. "I drew thee with the bands of love, yet thou knowest not My healing." Even the stones will sing if you praise them. Many an inactive organ within you needs the oil of your praising to set it into happy action. This is what Jesus Christ teaches me. Why, what a simple lesson it is! Praise! This is where you become like Jesus Christ, then your principle of action will win. Rest and Freedom are names of Jesus Christ.

A sperm whaler believed in the Sabbath as God's rest for his men. He, as captain, refused to have his men work on the Rest Day. The mate threatened to have him dismissed. "God will be justified," he said. Then an awful hurricane came up, and down the mate got in terror, but the captain smiled and drew into a port where they never thought of such a thing as a cargo, but they got a full cargo in one-third the time.

How can we help loving God?

"All my trust on Thee is staid.

All my help from Thee I bring,

Cover my defenseless head

With the shadow of Thy wing."

Spurgeon" called $43,000 per year to his orphanage by asking God. That is the greatest honor you can pay the true God — the "one God above you and through you and in you all" — give Him the glory for everything.

And the gates of hell are nothing against your fortress where God, the true God, is praised as the sender of all your blessings.

Another man saw the sweet freedom Jesus Christ had by having God so reign in Him, and he opened his art collection and hired a band for the villagers to come to his house Sunday evenings. The pious ones were horror stricken, but somehow, he remembered how Jesus Christ told the man to carry his bed home one time when even to wear heavy shoes was against the sabbatical law of carrying burdens and also bruised corn when even to walk in grass was prohibited. He saw that freedom was a name of God, not bondage to notions.

So when a gale of financial stress struck his business what did those villagers do but rise like one man to help him out?

You see there is a principle of goodness that is better than regulations of man. Recreation is rest. Freedom is rest. God is rest. The true God makes you kind, merciful, trustful. This is life eternal to your hope, to your joy, to your friendships, to your loving. There is nothing to hate. You forgive everybody and everything. You give for the ugly pain a loving word; "I forgive you." To the sharp circumstance; "I forgive you." You have a reservoir of healing oil that you pour over the affairs of your daily lot, in "I forgive everybody and everything." Nothing to hate. Did you suppose there was any merit in your hating tobacco and rum?

Tell them that you forgive them. They will lose their stings. The sting of them is your hate. You have the power to take up any deadly thing and it shall not hurt you. Cannot God touch God and be undefiled? All is God. Hate nothing. The attraction of everything is God. Now that you know this, you will not be hurt by any of these things any more, will you? "The Truth shall make you free."

Today Jesus Christ prays for some in particular. Dear hearts, now and then you must be very, very definite in telling whom you would have especially blessed and naming your particular request. Jesus Christ did this. God is not above helping you out of the tiniest little troubles. The buttercup is as softly painted as the tulip. Your blessing —

name it at the foot of the throne within the Holy Place of your mind.

"It shall be done unto you." And God shall wipe away your tears, and heal your heart. Today you may tell what you would like best for your beloved in your home.

"I pray for these today,

My heart folds these today.

Speed busy world today.

For these I pray today."

November 15, 1891

LESSON VIII

JESUS AND JUDAS

John 18:1-13

Here there are two central characters figuring out the chief idea of human life. Jesus and Judas standing for the praise of prosperity. Prosperity or satisfaction is the chief aim of every creature that lives. Judas stands for the idea of getting prosperity by worldly methods, unspiritual, prosaic. He praises success. His very name means praise of success.

"Get money," he says, "honestly if you can, but get money." Jesus stands for the idea of prosperity by spiritual law, confidence in God, idealistic methods.

"There is but one way given under heaven," He says. His very Name means praise or success in understanding of the principle of goodness. There comes a time in the experience of every mind, every organized body, and the planet also when the two ideas are face to face, and here you see the

demeanor of each and the merits of each with the prophesy of each standing boldly out on the canvas of human life.

Caiaphas means depression of spirits, or pessimism. Annas means the common lot of humanity as seen daily. Malchus means the outward action of Caiaphas and Annas, or how they act when given reign. Anarchy, nihilism, communism are the soldiers of the pessimism that steals over the mind of a man or planet when it has been conferring with Judas as to how to be successful in life.

As Jesus faced Judas, so the two plans of the planet are met today in face-to-face issue. God is my prosperity, or gold (the symbol of God) is my prosperity. Which? "My mind to me a kingdom is." When I settle the question for myself, I am either mastered by Jesus or Judas.

The planet has its nations, its tribes and peoples, which are its thoughts. Today it is called to settle the question of how it shall secure its highest good, or its prosperity.

There is a spiritual sphere enfolding and penetrating and permeating the planet. Above all and through all and in all is Spirit, lying close and filling full, as substance to shadow.

Every now and then somebody breaks out of the shadow and speaks from the sight of the substance. Sir Thomas Browne said, "The severe learning of the schools shall not take from me the idea that everything upon the earth is but the shadow of some substance lying nigh it."

Milton said, "What if the earth be but the shadow of heaven and things thereon each like to other more than on earth they seem?"

Balthazar the Egyptian is made to say, "There is a kingdom on the earth, though it is not of it; a kingdom wider than the bounds of the earth, though they were rolled together as finest gold and spread by the beating of hammers; its existence is a fact, as our hearts are facts, and we journey through this kingdom from birth to death without seeing it, nor shall any man see it until he hath known his own soul."

It is told by those who have shaken off the slumber of the shadow enough to speak plainly, that to look into this kingdom is to be free from all the bondages of earthly ways.

They tell us that we may not seem to our neighbors and friends to be different in form or color or speech from themselves, yet that we may have the light of that Kingdom in our eyes and the knowledge of that Kingdom in our heart so truly that the promise of the Bible may be fulfilled in us, *"when thou passest through the waters I will be with thee, and through the rivers they shall not overflow."*

"When thou passest through the fires they shall not burn thee, neither shall the flame kindle upon thee." "At destruction and famine thou shalt

laugh." "Ye shall know the truth and the truth shall make you free."

Those who examine the shadows carefully, viz., the material universe, dispute the possibility of such things. They tell us we must not get too ideal in the face of facts. Their eyes are fixed steadily upon the seeming processes, and their hearts are heavy because the long night of sorrow, treachery, and dying promises no quick dawning, if indeed there ever is to be any change in nature's performances.

Among these there is always some John of the Apocalypse promising that in a far-off future there surely will be "no death, neither sorrow nor crying; neither shall there be any more pain, for the former things have passed away." But the sight of the shadows causes Schopenhauer to declare that there is no God, only a "gigantic evil evolving into good." He sees the sight of evil stretch so far ahead that there is only hopelessness in his heart.

What is the matter with Schopenhauer and his followers? They have conferred with. Judas. They lived and longed for prosperity. They had a right to prosperity. But they should have conferred with Jesus.

Jesus said, *"Seek first the Kingdom of God, and all these things (riches, and honors, and health, and love, and gladness) shall be added unto you."*

Judas had told them that while they are in the
world they must look to the world's way and meet
it in its own fashion if they would be successful.

After conferring with Judas, hear the verdict of
the boldest and most intrepid magazine of our age
representing the summing up of the conclusions of
centuries: "Europe is cankered and honeycombed
with pessimism."

(Caiaphas was high priest that same year.)

"It needs no very long stay in Europe to detect
a strange drooping of spirit."

"Neither Pope nor church, peace societies nor
alliances can check its course."

"Schopenhauer and Von Hartman, with their
black pessimism, lead the continent."

"Nothing in fiction or music is believed in by
the world now", they add, "except pessimism."
Optimistic teachings are not listened to.

"Wagner, St. Beauve, Carlyle, Matthew Arnold, Scherer, Tolstoi and Ruskin are under the
evangel of bafflement and despair."

Metaphysics has caught the echo and assures
us of a great unconscious movement of evil besides
the apparent.

If you give Ruskin his sleep and his food and
his shelter and his police defenses of the best, you
can not secure him from having his brain pum-
meled so that it will show how the invisible action

of mind upon mind in deadly apposition can manage his destiny.

If the father is unjustly severe in his thought against his child it will have brain fever or diphtheria. "We wrestle not against flesh and blood, but against principalities, against powers against the rulers of darkness", says the metaphysician, who has conferred with Judas. "Be not afraid, I have overcome the world." "Your joy no man taketh from you." "Thou couldst have no power at all except I gave it thee." "All power is given unto Me." "I am in heaven," "Where I am there ye may be also." This is the conclusion of those who refuse to confer with Judas as to the best means of being successful, that even the earth and the fullness thereof are seen to be their own birthright.

All the forces of bafflement meet Jesus the teacher of spiritual law today. They feel angered against ideality and optimism.

And Jesus says, "Whom seek ye?" The drill sergeant answers, "The Nazarene." That is, "that *ignis fatuus* (a misleading influence or thing) promise of God that has claimed to be something but is nothing." "I Am He!" The "He" is not in the Greek, and all those who stood by understood Jesus to speak from the highest Son of Man or Son of God — the God-man standpoint — I Am God "I Am;" to them all was the name of Jehovah.

Some have contended that Jesus did not speak of Himself directly as God. They give away their ignorance of Greek by so saying. Here He meant to show man's idea to be God's idea, when man pro-claimed his highest.

Their idea of man was limited to their study of the shadow side. "Our days upon the earth are as the shadow that declineth;" we are "worms of the dust," was their doctrine. The common lot is sor-row.

His idea of man was of one with dominion over all things, death and starvation included; master and king and lord through spirit instead of subject and slave and cringing subject through believing in the power of matter over man. When He said "I Am," the soldiers and officers immediately went backward and fell on their faces. The pessimist always falls back when the Christ faith looks him in the eye. In supreme moments many a man and woman has felt the God power rise and swell and burst forth. Eliza can take her baby across impos-sible ice floats.   The Red Sea divides.   All these things become possible. "Is anything too hard for Me?" A good man in a lonely mountain pass was assailed by lawless ruffians. As they came forward the glory of a Supreme Power sprang forth from him. It spoke through him. It was Him. "You can not! I am God!" They fell back aghast. But then, as in this case they sprang forward again. "We will kill you for saying that." But as he looked at them, they fled.

"Because thou being a man maketh thyself God."

At each stop of your way "keep My words" and you will step out free from all these experiences I am taking. When pessimism, hardships, violence, threaten you, announce your spiritual nature at its highest. I AM! Jesus is very sure of victory for the spiritually taught.

"Let them go." He tasted all this hour which tempts your own mind and the mind of the planet. He knew His power through the Word. If we keep His words we will step into freedom.

No other teacher ever gave us a sure recipe for safety in time of danger, or for health in place of sickness. Plato said the world needed a teacher who should show man how to be master instead of subject. He had carefully noted that Socrates did not help him to master his environments and destiny.

Here you and I are shown that within the self is one thought that if it be given utterance poverty and sorrow and failure will be no more.

Why should we let other thoughts come up and argue with us to prove our powerlessness when that one announced would prove our power? What an affirmation is demanded of man when Annas and Caiaphas and Malchus, incited by Judas, face him!

Hold your own! Hold on to the great Word! All the thoughts of the mind must join forces with the bold affirmation Jesus teaches.

All things you would see brought to pass wait the rise and swell and glory of the God within. Therefore, come boldly up and be steadfast. All matter quails. The earth is clean dissolved. Prospero shows that he had his thoughts under control, so that he could calm or enrage the seas at his will; but he knows not Jesus Christ. All to him is but the "baseless fabric of a dream" — easily dissolved. He was right, but he had nothing better to turn to. You have. Speak boldly.

"Boldness hath genius, power and magic in it.

What you can do, or dream you can, begin it."

Let the old ways be dissolved like a breath when you speak from the true power you already possess. The true keeper of the words of Jesus Christ is the true Christian. As a Christian you must expect miracles. If you do not believe in miracles take off the name Christian.

"Either change your name or honor it," said Alexander to a soldier named for him who had acted ignobly.

Ask much of the principle you serve. Ask richly, "He remembers that I am a king and should give like a king. Honor his claim," said a king of one who had asked so great a gift that the treasurer was afraid.

You must expect to open prison doors, feed the nations, raise the dead. The King you serve is Jesus Christ in you, conqueror over all things. The Emperor Theodosius liberated his prisoners and cried out, "Would God I could open the graves and set those captives free."

"Place no limitation on yourself," says the spirit of this lesson. Notice that Jesus Christ stood still at the place of His capture and set His people free. He stood still where He was and quelled the solders. He stood still where He was and healed the ear of Malchus. He stood still preaching when the officers could not take Him. He hung still on the cross and saved the thief.

Right here is the spot where you are called to live and work — here is your place to demonstrate dominion.

"Away, says the fiend. Rouse up a brave mind, says the fiend and run. No, my honest friend Launcelot Gobbo, being an honest man's son, budge not! Budge, says the fiend.

The fiend gives me more friendly counsel. I will run, fiend. My heels are at your commandment. I will run."

This is the plausible reasoning of those thoughts that would argue that you could do better in some other field than the one where you are.

What saith Scripture? *"Stand thou in thy lot till the end of the days."* Till what belongs to you to do there is finished.

"Breathe California spices,

Roll blue Pacific waves,

Here ope the paradises,

Here close for us the graves."

Felix of Nola, being hotly pursued, fell into a cave near at hand, and the spiders wove a web across it and the dews fell on it and on went his pursuers. Right there where you are, set the people free. Why should a thought within you depress you or discourage you? Are you not master within your own realm?

When depression at the sight or feeling of your own hard lot or that of theirs seizes you, announce your Jehovahship. Then you can handle your own thoughts.

Would you like to tell the law to stop making it possible for one man to own $150,000,000, while his next-door neighbor can hardly feed his children?

You can set that right in the world if you can site it right in your own mind first. The ideal of equal rights and equal opportunities is a Christian one. And Christ shall reign from sea to sea, and from the river to the uttermost parts of the earth.

You are the result of your own arguments, but you need not be the result of anybody else's arguments.

"Though all around thee courage fail.

Do thou be strong.

Though all around thee doubt prevail.

In faith move on!"

"Put up thy sword," said Jesus. And He healed the anarchist. They tell us that in Europe there is nothing heard of but "smokeless powder, small-bore rifles, heavy ironclads, swift cruisers, torpedo boats, and dynamite guns." France and Germany have 6,000,000 soldiers armed to the teeth.

If any Christian Peter thinks to meet anarchy and nihilism with the world's weapons he is as foolhardy as Peter. "The weapons of our warfare are not carnal but mighty through God to the pulling down of strongholds." "Put up thy sword."

You need not describe the cancer spots of city life, nor scold the ministers for not going down into their midst and knowing what is going on.

Your own thoughts of powerlessness are all your accusations amount to. If you believe they can be cured you are the one who can cure them. Did God invest any minister of the gospel with more power or more opportunities than He invested you with? No! God is no such God.

You have no right to expect anybody to do what you are not already doing, and can not teach them how to do.

I Can! and I Am! is your affirmation. You do not need the city government, police force, nor public sentiment on your side; all you need is the agreement of your own thoughts.

"Shuffle off the mortal coil" of your own thoughts.

Give all thoughts the lie except that one which says, "I can stream like a flood of glory down into the dark places with my limitless omnipotent love, and I can feed and warm and love them. And I can go like an angel of goodness to the hearts of the banqueters and tell them how the God of them — the Christ in them — loves to give of their substance of their love, their wisdom. So I will tell them till I see the rich and the poor meet at one common table of knowledge of their own birthright of all things."

Did you suppose God is less God in the high gambler than in Jesus? No. But Jesus announced it boldly. If you do not declare your goodness and power and divinity, how shall you measure whether the gambler is worse or better than you? All he has done is to let his thoughts not divine, parley with the highest ideal just as you have. He has listened to the Judas idea that he must practice the world ways to be successful. Have you ever parleyed in that way? Over the turbid waters of Cedron walked Jesus into the garden of peaceful thought.

Stop not to argue with the worldly wise, or the ways of the shadow. Look over them all into the peace country that is all around you.

The parched earth traveler shall be glad when he hears this doctrine that when he lets this I AM speak, his vain thoughts must fall back, and his bread and his milk and his honey shall never more fail.

The pale mother may feel the reviving airs of the hilltops of heaven blow across her brow with refreshment. She shall set her tired feet into the beautiful country where there shall be no more pain, neither sorrow nor crying, when she knows that within her own soul is the key to glad living here and now by speaking the words that are true.

Therefore, let the high thought be born in whomsoever these teachings are received.

"In the beauty of the lilies Christ is born across the sea,

With a glory in His bosom that transfigures you and me."

November 22, 1891

LESSON IX

SCOURGE OF TONGUES

John 19:1-16

"Pilate took Jesus and scourged Him." But Jesus said never a word. We do not speak when the scourge of tongues is upon our character, our work, our motives.

We do not think anything when the scourge of adversity is upon our undertakings. We do not think or speak when sharp pains scourge our bodies. We answer never a word when one who has wronged us sorely tries by adroit accusings to make us speak some retaliatory words to engage us in quarrel. We give the "soft answer that turneth away wrath" when one has come to feel that he has just cause for anger against us. Thus is the summary of this lesson.

According to the Gospel of Jesus Christ, all evil is a lie from the beginning — pure delusion. But the loving kindness of the Gospel is such that we may know exactly what to do under every circumstance and condition of human experience to rise out of suffering which seems real. According to the Gospel, suffering of any kind was not made for the children of God; and we are the children of God.

Jesus told us that if the cup of sorrow should be pressed to our lips we must refuse it, saying: "I will not drink it, I refuse it." He tasted it once for the purpose of telling us we need not drink it. He showed us we need not drink it. He showed how the refusing to feel sorrowful at a sorrowful state of affairs would set the affairs straight.

This is the Gospel. Under the law and the prophets we have cause and effect, physical and metaphysical.

Under the law we have the cold to chill our bodies into consumption and the failing mental state to show a wrong thought once held.

Under the Gospel, *"None of these things move me."*

At each point of human experience touch your lot -with the Gospel and be free from cause and effect.

The oldest teaching known to the race is that all things we see and feel and hear and taste were wrought and built by some thoughts we used to hold.

We have now riches or poverty, health or sickness, sorrow or gladness, friends or foes, according as our thoughts have formulated. Edwin Arnold gives us this as the teaching of Buddhism ;

"Thought in the mind has made us.

What we are by thought was wrought and built.

If a man's mind hath, evil thoughts,

Pain comes to him as comes the wheel the ox behind."

Once they taught in ancient books that we are surrounded by a cosmic ether or matter principle which receives every thought we think and every word we say and brings it forth as the soil brings up the seeds.

Some thoughts are slow to come to fruit, just as some seeds are slow. The apple seed is longer than corn; the corn longer than the pea.

Every affirmation is a prayer. An affirmation is a positive statement that something is. Every affirmation carries the tacit asking for something and also carries the tacit expectation that it will be so proved. A certain quick-tempered feeling, for instance, is the tacit asking for something bad to happen. We speak impulsively the, affirmation, "You are a hateful thing." We, of course, expect something to result from our speaking: either the pain or the despair of somebody.

Then we forget our word, but afterwards we are lame or some member of our family is disabled, "For the lightest word thou shalt give account in the day of judgment." Judgment is when the words have come forth in solid pictures.

There is a physical mode in trying to set things that are consequences right. The oculist, the artist, and the surgeon are as busy as can be rectifying consequences. Our popular magazines often have page after page of descriptions of successful management of consequences by surgeons, artists, oculists.

But the metaphysician or moralist says so long as the causes remain, the consequences will follow as "comes the wheel the ox behind," If a strong prejudice caused cataract, the cataract will stay till the prejudice is gone; it will form and reform, says the moralist. If Napoleon III shoots causelessly at Maximilian in Mexico, Napoleon's son must be shot causelessly in the jungles of Africa.

For every shriek of the drowning slave thrown overboard to lighten the slave ships in the storms, a Harvard boy, a Yale youth or a farmer's son must fall on the battlefield of the Republic in the civil war that sets them free.

From Genesis to Revelation, *"Eye for eye and tooth for tooth"* for everybody and everything out of Christ. The cheating of the car-conductor out of your fare, though you argue that the corporation is rich and you are poor, will put you behind sixty and an hundred fold more than the fare.

Confidence in the God of right will add to you sixty and an hundred fold, "He that leadeth into captivity shall be led into captivity, and he that killeth with the sword, shall be killed with the sword," whether it be sword and bondage of tongue or steel.

To annul this we follow Christ Jesus. We cannot make believe follow His ways, either. Making believe brings failure and loss. "The hypocrite's hope shall perish." Here is a beautiful lesson in Christ of how to act under the stings of the tongue of the law, when we are in some bodily torture or mental pain, or hurting circumstance. Keep still. There is a breathing finer than the nostrils and the lungs and the airs experience. There is a pulse beat more irresistible, and a heartbeat for ever steady, which it is impossible to watch with the muscles relaxed and the mind intent. When the little widows of India were asked how they endured the scourgings of their lot one of them explained that they had learned that they had a finer life within them which would live and bear it, if they would be still enough. Shall we not see the Christ in the innocent victims? Is not the Christ able? Is not Christ in us? This is the finer life that can make scourgings nothing if we relapse into it.

Within the alchemy of mind is the peaceful Spirit. Within the chemist's fire is the crystal ice. Within the sun, a center of peace. Within the cyclone, stillness. Within mind, God. *"My peace I give unto you."* That finer life within us all knows no suffering; knows no death never heard of any of them. We all have the same faculty given us of watching the subtle, sweet life when the pains and

torments of our past thoughts come to their fruit-
age, and thereby not feeling the pains.

We may call it the faculty of wrapping the
mantle of our own thoughts around us, as we are
taught in science to do on the Sabbath.

Indeed, the teachings of Jesus are the twelve
simple lessons of Christian science put into practi-
cal living. The silent life of us is the triumphant
power of us. It will speak and live so perfectly for
us, we get into the way of letting it, that we see
and hear and know only that life, and to us it is no
longer silent.

In these days of noise and hurry we must not
lose sight of that fine victorious life ever coursing
through us, willing to do all things for us.

In a newspaper we were all told lately that
everything nowadays has to be loudly heralded,
"To depend upon merit is obsolete and chimerical
(No existence except in thought). The only winning
card is assurance." But Jesus Christ's teachings
were for all time and for every situation. He
taught a sure rule for success. Success means good
health, good judgment and prosperity. All other
ways except His way have failed. Let us try His
way.

"The letter fails and systems fall,

And every symbol wanes;

The Spirit overbrooding all.

Eternal love remains."

88

Try for your health the silent way, the supremely still way. A few years ago a number of invalids, scourged, beaten things they were, had an idea come to them all over the world simultaneously, as an idea of a patent car-coupler would strike ten thousand minds just ready for it simultaneously. They determined to be still — still — still, and see what would become of them. They all got well. How many have stopped their vain searchings and hard studying to suddenly find themselves thoroughly enlightened on the subject that had baffled them, *"Be still and know that I Am God."* You can get best financial and professional success by relying upon the still principle.

"Serene, I fold my hands and wait,

Nor care for wind or tide or sea.

I rave no more 'gainst time or fate, For lo! My own shall come to me."

Some people will not turn to the silence of the fine life within them till they are driven by the winds of sore failure of every other plan. There is a wind flower in South America which will not show its sweet bloom unless the rough winds blow, but we need not wait for calamity to blow sore winds, or the scourging of pain. We may sing the Benedictus from a silence not enforced like Zachariah's. We need not wait for the law to imprison us before we write a great book like Bunyan. Here we are taught to cease from fretting at sore trials for they simply mean that old ways of thinking and old material conditions are being struck off.

We have got into set ways of thinking, supposing feeling. When we have believed in the necessity for summer and winter, seed time and harvest, we have come to believe in toil — hard toil. If we believe in hard toil we believe in unavailing toil this always brings death or famine to the individual and to the planet. Death of peace, hope, substance, happiness, friends — death of something.

"As comes the wheel the ox behind."

Pilate, whose name shows that he stands for a hand of the law and the prophets, finds no real fault in us. He is simply an instrument of the people with some hint of a soul. He lays all the blame of the scourging onto somebody else. His wife warns him.

Whoever acts the Pilate will be warned in advance.

Before you speak harshly to your boy for some supposed offense, stop. You had a warning not to do it by a feeling the other day that something bad was going to happen to him. You are the thing that is going to happen to him. The child must not be scourged by your tongue or our ships, for Pilate acted out always has a fearful end.

"Take ye Him," said Pilate. Now be no coward. If it was right for Pilate to scourge Jesus it was right for him to finish the punishment. The Adam type never likes to be responsible. The Christ always is. Bold, intrepid people have more admiration from us than shrinking, shirking ones,

Cortez wins our admiration, though his boldness was engaged to ignoble uses. We see how he was a hand of the law, not afraid to destroy those Aztecs in a religious frenzy as those Aztecs had boldly destroyed twenty thousand noble youths every year in cruel religious frenzy. Cleopatra was intrepid, fearless to the last breath.

"We have a law," shouted the populace, *"whereby He ought to die."* This law was Lev. 24:16, which put their neighbors to death for blasphemy. But who should judge what is blasphemous?

Luther haughtily refused to shake the hand of the gentle Zwingli because he thought the kindly heart had blasphemed God. But is haughtiness honor of God? Is not mercy and tolerance more Godlike? How can the Presbyterians, Episcopalians, Catholics, etc. know whether they or the Briggs, Newtons, Brooks, McGlynns, etc., are more nearly Godlike, save by the mercy, gentleness, love, forgetfulness of opinions they show? Who is more likely to be honoring the Maker of all things, he who calls himself a worm of the dust, a helpless child, or He who rises and says, *"All power is given unto Me in heaven and in earth, for I and my Father are One?"*

The Pilate nature is in great doubt when he gets between the two factions, one calling himself a helpless infant and the other God in His Greatness. "Whence?" But Jesus answers nothing, for Pilate is determined not to hear the Jesus idea. He is mortally afraid of the people. Do not explain yourself to one who is afraid the people are not ready to be told of their omnipotence and omniscience. Your silent presence is all they can bear.

Whatever you know of your power and wisdom will treat them. They will catch the idea from your atmosphere. If you said yesterday to anything, "I hate it," or "I hate you," somebody coming near to you today will feel a little hate of you come suddenly into his mind. You cannot think a thought but somebody will catch it, and if your mind is absolutely absorbed with any theme everybody will catch it.

So you see how the disease germs will spread by thinking of disease germs. You see how a doctor may actually drop down into your house the idea of that last case he attended and you will be another just like it on his list pretty soon.

To study nosology, classification of disease, astrology, causes of disease, symptomatology, symptoms of disease is not nearly as healthy a state of mind to carry around as the absorption - with the idea. "The Spirit maketh you every whit whole." Now Pilate gets angry. What at? Why, because he has done Jesus a great wrong, and His patience under it makes Pilate hate Him.

Rosina Vokes in one of her plays says, "I have done him a great wrong and I hate him for it?" The audience laughs knowingly when she repeats the little truism of the Pilate type.

Here is where Jesus speaks. Pilate begins to feel it was cruel of Jesus to get him into such a predicament. *"Pilate,"* He says tenderly, *"you would not have done it if you had acted out your own best judgment."* There is no real power in being wrong even with members on your side. Power is in being in the right. He shows him how his foolishness came from Judas, the luster. Weakness had its rise in lust of some kind. So, whoever is cowardly or weak or faltering of courage of mind or body needs the whole six treatments of science.

Pilate refused the divinity side and gave over to the material side of the question. All those who parleyed with Judas ended violently. They had to, because they kept under the law of cause and effect, as "he that killeth shall be killed."

Judas, Pilate, Herod, Caiaphas, Annas, where are they? How ended they? Jesus and His doctrine — were they crucified, killed? To the Christ that never was crucified, to the Christ that never was entombed, to the Christ that never had to rise, being already risen, to the triumphant Christ, high over principalities and powers and nations, be joined. Ye are of like Substance. The fine, still life within you, watch it: it is Christ within you, victorious over all, never knowing defeat of health, or wisdom, or wealth,

November 29, 1891

LESSON X

SIMPLICITY OF FAITH

John 19:17-30

"He, bearing- His cross, went forth into a place called the place of a skull." The history of Jesus Christ is the history of one who, knowing that He owns great possessions, takes upon Himself the estate of the lowliest people, not to give to them as if they were objects of His charity, but to teach them how to have as much as He has.

He is the history of one who takes upon Himself all kinds of sicknesses to teach sick people how to get well. He is the history of one who takes the deepest grief upon Himself to teach us how to rise out of it. He is the history of one who teaches how to get very wise and successful while being ignorant and unfortunate. In other words, He bore the cross of the world.

If He, being rich, had given large provisions to the poor, He would have been a failure. If He, being powerful, had simply healed a few and lifted

up a few and enlightened a few, He would have
been as great a failure as those powerful people
who condescended in the time of the cholera in
Naples. A very rich man rode among the poor people in his carriage carrying broths and medicines,
but they were so enraged at him, that they
mobbed him, broke his carriage in pieces, tore the
harness off his horses, and nearly held a riot in the
city. King Humbert went among them, dressed
just like one of them, helped them nurse their sick
and bury their dead, and they never touched him,
though they knew that he was richer than the
other man.

This was because he did not flaunt the difference of his position in their faces. Now, if King
Humbert had told them that they might as well
have sixty and an hundred fold more possessions
than they had, and explained it to them how they
might be as powerful and well fed as himself, it
would have been something like what Jesus Christ
did.

He bore your very experiences and told you the
exact way out of them. He was offered money and
houses and castles and kingdoms if He would take
the world way of getting them. He was shown how
able a financier He was by nature; how able a
ruler He would make; how noble He would appear
as a prince, and if He would deal the world's way
He could over-top even the Caesars.

He saw that He had magical healing powers;
that He could perform all the mighty tricks of

legerdemain Solomon had excelled in. It had been considered that Solomon was wonderful, because he could pierce a delicate pearl, string intricately perforated diamonds, and answer peculiar conundrums. All this was so simple and easy for the young Jesus.

But he said, "I will not get my greatness that way, I will get wise in the knowledge of Spirit, I will get all my powers from God in straight communion with God, and not till I can explain how God as the Father is impartially good to all the children of men will I take any of the goods of earth."

"I believe in God as able and willing to do all things that mankind can ask or even think. I do not believe in there being any poor people or old people or unhappy people. I believe God is good to all or that He is not good at all. I do not believe in ignorance, I do not believe in failure. I do not believe in dishonesty. These things are not necessary. There is a noble, satisfactory way of living. That way I will demonstrate in such fashion that not one creature can be too ignoble to imitate."

And he did. The seemingly heavy human affairs that despite the goodness of God He bore and said, *"Be not afraid; I have overcome." "The flesh profiteth nothing." "The devil is a lie from the beginning." "Keep My words." "My words are Life." "My words tell the power of Spirit. Seek first the knowledge of God and all these things shall be added unto you that you desire."*

He said God was in Him. He said God was and is in all. He said that this God in each of us is able and willing to help us in wonderful ways. Nothing is too hard for Him, He explained that nothing is too commonplace for us to lay before this God and get aid.

He said that He Himself was the bodily demonstration of God. But He laid great stress upon the fact that just talking and thinking as He did (being absolutely right) would put Him and His powers forth from each of us.

A very poor woman not very long ago felt that she heard the voice of Jesus Christ speaking within her mind saying, "I am Jesus Christ." She said, "Yes, I know, but I do need help so much! Won't you please help me pay my rent?" The voice within her mind never said "Yes." She listened to her own mind and so gently and lovingly the same words came, "I am Jesus Christ!"

If she had let this voice speak aloud through her lips her neighbors would have said she was blasphemous. But she did not. She said again, "Yes, dear Jesus Christ, I know you are the highest thought of my mind — able to do all things, won't you please help me pay my rent?"

And again all she could get was the affirmation stronger and fuller from the deeps of her own mind. And immediately after that she had help on her way. "Ye shall ask what ye will in My Name."

According to Jesus Christ you do not have to ask any man or woman or corporation to help you; Jesus Christ will attend to it. Not the historic Man of Galilee but the omnipotent Jesus Christ quality of your own mind.

Jesus Christ is the demonstration of good. Just to listen to the one thought that whispers within you is your demonstration.

It is not right for you to be poor. It is not right for you to be sick. It is not right for you to fail. It is not right for you to be unhappy. Why will you be when Jesus Christ says, *"I am within you able to do all things. Nothing is too hard for Me. Do not look afar unto Me, but let My Name be spoke within you, and love Me and believe in Me."*

You can do everything when Christ Jesus is your chief word. By and by the world will not seem heavy to you. You will not be Atlas with the world on his shoulders, but Jesus with the world under His feet. Your whole business in life is to "learn of Me," or to learn how to let the Jesus Christ thought within you reign supreme. This thought that is named Jesus Christ is the noblest thought within your mind. Let it keep saying "I am Jesus Christ." Tennyson kept repeating his own name till he felt as if he was as big as the planet. Some mystics kept repeating certain syllables, but Jesus Christ said, "Repeat My Name." Then you will not feel as if you were the planet but as if the world

were under your feet. You will not become senseless, like the mystics who repeat senseless
syllables, by speaking My Name, but will come
into your inheritance of health, wisdom, and success.

The place of a skull was where they crucified
Him. Your intellect is supposed to be located
within your skull. This intellect is a great enemy
to Jesus Christ, "The natural man receiveth not
the things of the Spirit". One has to walk right
over the words and teachings of the intellect just
as Jesus did. There is a higher faculty than the
intellect within you. It is Spirit, intellect is more
powerful than muscle. It is more successful than
muscle. Intellect is as unreliable, however, as
muscle. The powerful intellect will tell us that we
must not give to the worthy poor because if we
heed to every cry of pain we would soon be as poor
as the poorest. Spirit says, feed every one with a
portion of your bounty and you will have all the
more. Intellect says, I must put my money into
institutions that will praise my name and cut
down my employees afterward.

Spirit says, I must put every creature into the
way of earning its own living. If it cannot do the
way of the world, so much the more cause for my
protective care and wise instruction. I must not do
my alms to be seen of men. Honor among this generation counts for nothing. The future will read my
motive as clear as a book.

The intellect is proud over muscle. Spirit is proud over nobody and nothing, but far transcends all the powers of all the creatures. Intellect has its place in the skull. Jesus Christ has no place. Fills all place — unbounded, limitless, infinite.

Algazali, a pious Arabian, said he was completely astonished when he found how the senses deceived him, and his judgment had to be all corrected by his intellect. He noticed how the stars are reported to be small as money pieces by sensation, but corrected by intellect are called suns and worlds. He was of everything and everybody being sure different to the judgment from what the senses state. Then be began to doubt the reports of his intellect.

He said he was satisfied enough with his senses until intellect denied their testimony. Then he grew dissatisfied with intellect and wondered if there were not some higher faculty still that could correct it. Jesus here explains that He will teach us a higher than the greatest intellect.

Pilate, the representative of the world that acts according to its feelings, jestingly and willfully calls the spiritual teaching the ruling intention of Judaism.

The coward does the way of the world. He says the spiritual world is chimerical; says it claims to do everything, but so far as he sees does nothing.

Religious teachers try to explain that indeed they do not believe in spirit as their provider and healer and teacher. "We do the same ways you do; we try the tricks of all trades just like you; we believe in business ways and we employ doctors to examine our pulse and prescribe for our livers just like you; we study books as hard as ever we can to learn about God's laws with earthquakes and cyclones. Indeed, please, great worldly mind, don't think for a moment that we are so foolish as to believe in spirit." "Write not, King of the Jews."

But the world always will insist that it is the very nature of religion to teach a better way than material performances to be successful and happy.

There was no anguish you can go through with of mind or body, any greater than this great Jesus Christ took upon Himself to show you the words to speak to set you free.

Here He shows that if you feel anguish of mind or body you may be sure something good is coming to you. You can hasten its coming by saying, "It is finished." If you have been very sick and you let that thought within you speak, saying "I am Jesus Christ" and then you ask that thought to make you well, you will very likely have a very strange feeling of mind and body which no word will express better than anguish.

This feeling shows that a great good is to be born in you. Anguish gives us birth. You are to say, "It is finished. Jesus Christ took this cup and said I need not drink it. He said I might refuse it. So I refuse to be in anguish. I declare that what was meant for me is here now, according to Jesus Christ. I am perfectly well now."

Keep on speaking these words. You do not have to be put through any pain or sorrow or humiliation at all. But if you have got into these straits there is a quick way out.

Jesus Christ in you, the hope of glory, is your freedom. There is nobody so free as the one who lets this name be spoken within his mind. He finds that if he does not choose to go into the slums of the city to work he can help the people while sitting in his own room. He finds that if he does not choose to go into the slums he has a right to do so. He is under nobody's orders and nobody's criticisms weigh with him. He is not afraid of "the terror by night, nor the arrow that flieth by day,"

Criticism calumny, censure, praise, they are all one to him.

"It is finished," He says. Jesus Christ in you speaking tells you that all evil is finished. It is ended. These things shall not be upon the earth. You can speak this Name within your mind till the kingdom of heaven is open to your sight. In you the Gentiles will trust. As it is written "In My Name shall the Gentiles trust." That is, if you keep letting the Divine thought whisper within you, "I am Jesus Christ," even the people who do not believe in spiritual laws as transcending intellectual methods will trust you, will lean on you.

Jesus received the vinegar. But you need not receive the vinegar of having to take favors from the hands of those who have wronged you. He said to declare it as finished and to hold His Name steadfastly in mind would keep you free from all the pains and sorrows and shames of human experience. "I am victor over these things, in your mind first and then in your body and world."

There is salvation in none other name, but in My Name the vinegar and the gall and the wormwood of human experience are nothing. I promise you immunity from everything, if before you have got into trouble you will speak My Name. But if you have never been taught the power of My Name and are now in great anguish, say that you refuse the cup of trouble, and declare that "I in you am even now able to save you from poverty, debt, disgrace, desolation, sickness;" say, "It is finished." At the eleventh hour "call upon Me and I will hear." "Keep My Word and live." "I can not be crucified; I can not be entombed. Nothing is too hard for me." *"Now is the accepted time. Now is the day of salvation."*

December 6, 1891

LESSON XI

CHRIST IS ALL IN ALL

John 20:1-18

All over Christendom, when people use the expression which is the subject of this lesson, they mean to have us know that a principle supposed to have been dropped out of favor long ago is now come to the front as a power.

The idea which the dominant church supposed had been slain with Galileo is now risen smiling and calm as the orbit itself: a Christ is risen.

Did you reject it as absurdity when you first heard it spoken that visible material objects have, indeed, no reality as matter, but that as spirit is omnipresent their only substance is spirit, and therefore there is no matter? But now you begin to understand it, do you not? This is Christ risen again in you, the hope of glory. Your hope begins to be quickened, does it not? You have an indefinable expectation of something good coming to you from seeing the point, do you not? This expectation will not fail you. Truth never fails to bring something good to the one who recognizes her. Christ is Truth. Did you feel exceeding indignation when the metaphysicians not only insisted upon the unreality of matter, but also declared that all evil performances are only a delusion of the mind?

If you put the idea away and refused positively to entertain it, or consider it at all, then you rolled the stone of unbelief against the place where you hid the idea in your mind.

But the mind is very mysteriously retentive where a truth is concerned. Some day you will find that that idea is as clear as crystal to you. It rises smiling and loving and living as ever. There is not a truth you have ever heard spoken but what it is now milling within you and preparing to appear to you again. This is the nature of Truth. Then there are more intense statements of Truth than that evil is a delusion and matter is non est.

Mary Magdalene represents one who has cast out the seven false ideas of the human mind, and taken the seven right ones to replace them. You remember she had seven devils cast out by Jesus Christ. As Jesus Christ was strictly scientific in His mode of dealing with people, you can see He must have given her the seven noble affirmations of Truth to satisfy her mind with. Naaman washed seven times in Jordan to typify the seven cleansing words of mental law. The man mentioned by Jesus put out the seven devils or spirits or errors from his house or mind and neglected to receive the seven good words that belonged to him. It is to be expected that you will have put out these seven notions, viz., that there is any evil mixed with the omnipresent good in this universe where we dwell, and second that there is any matter or material thing in this universe.

You have learned that, strictly speaking, there is no absence of life, spirit, or intelligence. That there is nothing to hate, and that there is no reality in sin, sickness or death. You have also declared that there is no burden on your spirit or in your life, and have gladly put out of your mind the foolish idea that anything or anybody could get away from you anything that belongs to you. At first, very likely, these denials of what seems were rather hard for you to make, because all your past teachings and experiences belied them. But it is not at all a question of what we have been taught to believe, but a question of what is true.

Some people have been taught that they must live and think in a certain way or after they are dead they will be changed into bats and owls; but even if they believe it profoundly it will not be true. There are certain ways of believing which will make you nobly intelligent, perfectly healthy, and always successful. You are entirely dependent upon how much Truth you believe. The more Truth you believe the more successful you are. Failure along any line is sure evidence that you believe something that is not true very determinedly. If you have been failing in your undertakings you had better say very positively within yourself, "I hold no prejudice against anybody or anything in all the world." Such a message sent out of your mind will be sure to put the notion out of your mind which keeps you unsuccessful.

Only Truth is successful. If you answer me back that some liars are quite prosperous, I will point you to some great truth they do believe profoundly. Successful people generally laugh at certain notions you are hugging. All notions are prejudices against somebody or something.

All the regular denials of science have intenser exclamations of themselves. It was when Mary Magdalene had had the first statements of science, and had begun to speak them with deeper realization of them, that she is chronicled to have been found at the empty tomb, and to have spoken face to face with Jesus Christ.

For even the highest scientists there are still greater illuminations. Even the seven denials of science have harder statements of themselves. These harder statements operate with the advanced metaphysicians exactly the same as the first ones operate with those people who have believed in evil as a reality, in matter as having laws, and in sickness, misfortune and death as necessary adjuncts to existence.

The more metaphysical science you are acquainted with the more mastery you have over human conditions. Simple acquaintance therewith, however, is not high safety. Loving fellowship with them is the safety I am speaking of.

Often the highly scientific metaphysicians withdraw in horror from their colleagues when those colleagues make the denials of science over again according to their deeper meanings. They cry as Mary: *"They have taken away my Lord, and I know not where they have laid Him."* If they stand by, however, they will see the truth come face to face with a newer glory. It is not a good plan to run away and cut yourself off from your colleagues simply because they have spoken high science, just as it is not good for you to refuse the simple statements of science and roll a stone of unbelief against the door of the place in your mind where the statements are lying.

There is a noble principle involved in standing by and seeing the angels who have power to roll away unbelief. Angels are perfect thoughts — pure thoughts. They are the head and foot, the alpha and omega, of good. Your mind had better take them now in one Name, spoken while the joy of truth is not in you.

The joy of truth in you is when you realize that it was the true words you spoke that brought you this noble prosperity, and can see how exactly it will be so with you always. The angels are the words themselves, spoken faithfully because you have nowhere and nothing else to turn to but what you can say.

It is a pretty lonely time, seemingly, when you have nobody and nothing to turn to but your own prayers. But if you keep on speaking your faithful words you will find how they will turn you right around face to face with answered prayer.

Just one word is praying — or rather it is two words in one. This is the Name. Speak it. Jesus Christ. The words are alive. They will turn you into the right place, into the very arms of help.

A woman had been speaking this Name with all her might because so many things had happened which had desolated her mind and heart and life. Suddenly she stopped. Every one of the events changed in her judgment and before the day was out they had actually turned around so that they were better than she had even imagined.

Her home was saved. Her child was spared. Her undertaking was successful beyond description. Tolstoi says that it was actually taught by Jesus of Nazareth that in this life we shall have an hundred fold more prosperity than the world's people if we hold to Jesus Christ, but he mournfully looks at the poverty-stricken, feeble Christians and asks, "Do we?" If all those who have been prejudiced against prosperity, feeling it to be a snare of the devil, will turn right straight to what Jesus Christ taught, they will begin to make the denials of science and the affirmations of science, and instead of feeling their helplessness and inferiority and ignorance they will realize that their natural right is the dominion over the world, the flesh and the devil, which Jesus Christ had. To be owner of great possessions, to be wise in disposing of them; to be strong and buoyantly glad every minute, with the rich ability to teach all the rest of the world how to be so too, is the right of the Christian.

But if he be prejudiced against these things or prejudices his own fortune against them by trying to persuade people to love poverty and hug disease, he will never demonstrate his birthright. When you have once been brought to see how nobly rich the King's ministry is in reality you will hear your own name spoken. Ah! The name that is in your forehead, which is your keynote.

That name of yours is always with you. It is your secret recognition of the presence and office of Jesus Christ. You know Jesus Christ in your own way. You are not expected to know how Jesus Christ works with your neighbor to make him successful but you may know just exactly how Jesus Christ works with you to make you a transcendent delight.

When Jesus Christ said to Mary here, "Touch Me not." He meant to teach us that even when we are most rejoiced with what we have received we have not even then known the height and the depth, the length and the breadth of the riches of Jesus Christ.

We must keep on naming the Name. We must not stop naming the Name to watch phenomena of any kind.

To watch any phenomena as it looks to be is touching Jesus with human notions. Keep on naming the Name even if again for a season you do not see any sign of Jesus Christ in your lot but have only the memory of answered prayers.

Tell over what prayers you have had answered. Tell over and over -what great things you have had done for you. Jesus Christ is coming to abide with those who understand. The coming of Jesus Christ simply means understanding Truth. The abiding of Jesus Christ simply means the constant understanding of Truth.

Constant understanding of Truth has compelled those new statements of the metaphysics of life which are now demonstrating the freedom from all experience of pain, sickness, misfortune of those who make them. Suddenly the mind is illuminated to realize that there never was any such God as even the churches have described when most eloquently picturing Him forth. Suddenly it has been found that Jesus Christ is no such character as they tell us and had no such mission as they explain. Suddenly the whole fact looms up that mistaken teachings concerning God and Jesus Christ have built our prisons, waged our wars, pitted labor and capital against each other and given one home luxuries while the other starved.

Suddenly it is clear that the ministers in their pulpits, the moralists on their platforms, the Tolstois in their books, must stop their teachings and ask Jesus Christ what is true, regardless of what they have been taught was true, for Jesus Christ preached as life, health, strength, support, defense, just as the Name means, is risen never to go down behind the stone of unbelief in the hearts of those who have cried "Rabboni!"

December 13, 1891

LESSON XII

RISEN WITH CHRIST

John 21:1-14

"If ye then be risen with Christ, seek those things which are above," is the golden text of this lesson.

To be risen with Christ is to suddenly discover that you know a great truth about your own life as related to the God life. The instant we know such a truth we are changed in our bodies and in our minds.

There are statements of truth, glory beyond glory, and so there is no realization of what is true that has not a still higher realization in itself for us. Whenever Jesus Christ was with His disciples on the Sea of Galilee or Tiberias, you will notice how they are always closing out an old dispensation and beginning a new one, as in this case.

We all have our closing out of our old ways of thinking about Christ, as the church at large is always having its close of dispensations. There is a time when we must live on a higher plane from what we have hitherto been living on, or we shall deteriorate in every way. We are risen with Christ when we realize that there is a higher plane to think and live on than that we have been thinking and living on. We shall demonstrate new powers if we commence to live there the moment we see how it is. We are never where we do not come to such places. The Christian scientists have taken the highest statements concerning Christ that were ever taken, but they also find their times when they must rise to still higher statements of the same Christ. To refuse these risings with Christ is to deteriorate — to stop our prosperity.

A whole body of people may stop its prosperity along some line by not rising with Christ when somebody tempts them, or their pride or conservatism tempts them to take a lower view of life from what they see (dimly in the early morning, as the disciples of Jesus on Galilee) might be taken. Here the seven affirmations or two words embodied took the higher statements concerning Jesus Christ, viz., that He is not above doing the commonest favor for those who rise to accept His teachings.

Everything in this lesson has its exquisitely spiritual significance. It shows also how it is a sign of the acceptance of Christ from a higher plane when we can be fed and clothed and prospered by Him without feeling that it is demeaning Him any more than those people did who let Him help them at the time of this lesson.

Jesus Christ was Jesus of Nazareth, so full of understanding that there was nothing to Him, in Him, or of Him, except Christ or Truth. Whoever will be filled to overflowing with Truth, as Jesus was, will do as wonderfully as He, and be as much Christ as He. *"Where I am, there ye may be also."*

He never told people to do anything but what He Himself could do and did do. He said, *"Preach the gospel,"* and then preached so entrancingly that the very soldiers forgot to arrest Him, even when they might be executed for such neglect.

Ambition, that subtlest and strongest passion of man, was forgotten under the spell of His voice. "Man, proud man, dres't in a little brief authority" — glad to "play such fantastic tricks before High Heaven as make the angels weep," was tamed at the very moment when it was his chance to show his authority.

He told them to heal the sick and palsied hands, and leprous scales shone forth as wholesome flesh. "Multitudes came unto Him and He healed them every one" as easily as you would set a chair into its right place in your parlor or hang a picture straight on your walls.

He said, *"Cast out demons,"* and took Mary Magdalene and cast seven out of her, leaving her one of the noblest characters of history — last at His cross, most efficient at His embalming, weeping at His burial, first at His rising. The sin of the woman in adultery was erased. The man's heinous offenses were made nothing. The demoniac boy was set free.

He said, *"Raise the dead,"* And the daughter of Jairus, the widow's son, Lazarus and others came forth at His call to show that homes were never made to be decimated by death and we may unite all our families again if we will follow His teachings, rising to the acceptance of every new truth we hear which puts us farther away from the teeth of material laws and earthly experiences.

Last of all, He raised Himself, to show that we may never be so dead in any way, but that the Truth He told us will give us strength to rise full of quickened life as the solid dough rises with the quickening leaven.

He said that if we had His words in our mind, though we were dead yet should we live again. He said that if we should have His words already quickened within us we should never die — never even see death. Every single one of His works has been accomplished by some one or more of His disciples, except the self-raising. Not one has come forth into our sight after having been buried, and not one has proved his ability to live on and on indefinitely right here among us.

We must take into consideration how all truth has been received when spoken, to appreciate why no Christian has demonstrated protracted appearance among us. All of them had but newly come up out of the Egypt of materiality, and the smell of the smoke of the old ways was upon their garments while they were trying to tell how spiritual thoughts were capable of helping them out of all evil. Now and then they drooped and faded and fell from the reception their doctrine met. At the least sign of failure their neighbors and their families sneered. So they gladly, as Paul said, "preferred death rather than life," with such scorn at every step. Young in spiritual life is every Christian scientist. At their failures do not sneer.

"It is better to have tried and failed

Than never to have tried at all.

We are the work of Providence,

And more the battle's loss may profit those who lose

Than victory advantage those who win."

Here Jesus comes forth smiling and loving and healing as ever. For the third time He comes in substantial presence with substantial help. Christ is substance. Christ is substantial help. Believe this. You may have your shoes provided by Christ if you will rise to believe it. When a woman tells me she feels the power of the Spirit so strongly that the very cyclone stops when she speaks, I believe her and rejoice that she is risen into Christ of Truth. Why is she afraid to tell you this? When a woman or man tells me that she or he has received some financial assistance direct from God without a bit of intervention from human beings, why does my heart burn with delight as if I had conversed with one who had lately come from Jesus Christ on the banks of Galilee, while they would tremble at your peculiar smile or turning aside?

I suppose it is because I believe in the substantial, everyday friendship of Jesus Christ, and do not care at all about the harps and crowns and feathers of a faraway heaven.

"Christ dwelleth not afar. The King of some remoter star," to the disciple who has been fed and warmed under the shadow of the tender hills of Galilee.

Notice that He appeared to seven. Those seven are all named except two. You will often notice that two have no names when the risen Christ is near. Those of you who read the twelve lessons of Christian science will remember that there are five affirmations every mind on the planet ought to make, and then that each human being has two affirmations that belong to himself alone.

On the way to Emmaus (or to the knowledge that "they shall prosper that love God") two nameless disciples had Jesus with them. You will get Jesus Christ to warm your life with delight when you discover your own two. Please do not disapprove of your neighbor's two if he tells you them as very different from yours. You remember that to be a critic was formerly considered to be very smart, but that old dispensation has closed with the knowledge that criticism makes heart disease and sharp twinges of rheumatism. You have risen with Christ if you stop criticizing when you know the law.

Suppose your neighbor feels the God-power speaking so forcefully through him, that like Jeremiah, he says, "I am God and I make my world," all the time meaning the Spirit of himself and not the mortal at all. Will you let him use these two affirmations, even if your neighbor says he has not business with them, for his affirmations are, "I am Spirit and all my world is Spirit?"

These two affirmations not printed in the books have helped many. Try them:

1. "I am the friend of everybody and everything."

2. "I forgive everybody and everything."

You will find you are a reservoir of kindness that can warm the whole world. You can make everything lovely and blessed where you walk. You are bursting, overflowing with forgiving balms. You can pour oils over the troubled thoughts of the world. There is no limit to the conserved good within you that begins to demonstrate very soon after you start these two affirmations.

Here is a lesson of how sure Jesus Christ is to come to those who have just about got discouraged after trying very hard to believe that He is their helper and not seeing Him. Peter and Nathaniel and five others, finding they were objects of derision since their truth had met with what seemed ignominious defeat, made up their minds they would go back to their old business of fishing.

119

Often the very most spiritually-minded minister of God gets to feeling that maybe he has mistaken his calling because, in spite of his higher efforts, he has failed, and so concludes to go back to his old business. Here Jesus Christ gives him every bit of success that comes to him. At first he will toil unavailingly. Then when he has got discouraged in this also, and feels that it is a mystery whatever he was born for anyway, or why he is here, he makes a little lucky turn.

This is the Jesus Christ within him that has just got ready to act. This lucky turn is the casting of his net on the right side. Remember that there is not a single situation in which you can be placed that has not one little turn for you to make with it to make you absolutely successful.

This is the fourth dimension in space — or the Jesus Christ of you. All success shows the action of Jesus Christ. No matter on what plane you achieve success you are successful by the rising of the Jesus Christ within you.

Simon Peter drew in the net for them full to overflowing and yet the net did not break. Once before they had drawn in such a large netful that the net had broken. And this lake is the very place where Jesus found them on the very material plane of catching fish for their living in the first place. You see they were at the end of the material dispensation when Jesus called them first, and promised they should be fishers of men. And they were told by the second haul of fish, where their nets broke, that the first church that should come by their preaching should last a certain period, and should catch a very motley crowd and class of people, so that it would seem as if the Christian Church must break up and end by reason of such people as it would enroll upon its lists.

Under sanction of the church roll, men in high office might grind down the faces of the poor, and without censure prove unfaithful to the home. Under this dispensation men should believe in two powers — good and evil. They should believe in two beings — God and devil. They should believe in two personal characters, interceding and interfering with man — Jesus and Satan. Men should have their eyes so blinded as to which personality was dealing with them that they could not tell whether their actions were dangerous or safe, their thoughts powerful or weak. Just at the close of this dispensation they would not be able to turn to anybody or anything for help in health or happiness till they had cast their net on the right side — till they had done one little turn to help themselves.

Let me illustrate. In the streetcar the other day I saw a capitalist belonging to a church of the old dispensation shut the door crossly in the face of a little street-singer. Now that little face looking up was Jesus Christ. Some day that church member cannot recover the money he will lose till he has made his peace with Jesus Christ by doing something for the sake of that child. To do this would be casting his net for success in health and everything else, though it were at the eleventh hour.

Once a man told a good little Christian woman that if she would cure his boy he would give her a thousand dollars, but though the boy was cured he never paid anything to the laborer whose labor he had employed. He has lost $10,000. He will never recover the amount until he makes good his promise. Swedenborg saw that health comes to a time when the moral law must be observed in the heart and extend way into the actions or the body must lie down in a grave to begin the work over again. The old dispensation is closing when this law is heard of.

Then for those who have received that and come to an end of it, or lived it, there is the constant knowledge of only good — only God — only Jesus Christ, so that they have nothing to do but sit down and take the bread and fish Jesus Christ provides without questioning — just knowing "It is the Lord."

Sometimes people say of those who are determined to face the material world and the church of the old dispensation with the statement that there is but one Principle, one Presence, that if they should have pain or sickness or death or poverty in their home then they would find a principle of evil pretty real.

No. If they have these things they show that they believe now that evil is real and God owns a devil. "According to thy faith be it unto thee." They are under the old dispensation. This is the dispensation of supposition. The new dispensation supposes nothing. It knows in whom it believes, and its net never breaks. Its friends stand true to each other forever. Its families trust each other with a reason for the trust that is in them.

"Aunt Nancy you should be laying up some money for a rainy day," says a member of the old dispensation to the member of the new, "Suppose your employer should die, suppose you should have rheumatism; suppose — " "Stop!" says the colored believer in the new dispensation. "I neber s'pose nuffin', De Lawd is my Shepherd, an I shall not want. And honey, it's all yo' sposin' as is makin' yos so mis'able."

They shall hunger no more, neither thirst any more, under the last dispensation of the church where Jesus Christ is the daily provider acknowledged. "There shall be no more pain" when you have stepped out from under the yoke of the belief in sin and death into the freedom of the gospel that these things are all the results of supposing things that never could be true.

"The inhabitants shall not say, 'I am sick,' anymore," in all the earth where men hear the voice of Jesus on the shore at the close of their old ways of living, and make right restitution for the past and receive the gospel as it is in Truth.

You who are in trouble, failure, sickness, the old dispensation cries. Halt! The new dispensation

says, "Come, eat with Me." God is Good omnipresent, Love omnipotent, Spirit omniscient. There is
only God. Thus there is only Good.   There is only
Love.   There is only Spirit.   Do you believe there
is any opposite of God in the field of omnipresence?
Careful now, *"According to thy faith be it unto
thee."*

Do you not feel the circuit of the old faith closing and hear the voice of the new calling? Be risen
with Truth! "In that day there shall be one Lord
and His name One." "Do not I fill heaven and
earth?" "Is there any beside me? Nay, I know not
any."

December 20, 1891

LESSON XIII

THE SPIRIT IS ABLE

REVIEW OF YEAR

Six points are suggested to be considered by this lesson: temperance, the history of Jesus Christ as to His birth, His preparation for His ministry, His teaching as a whole and the particular doctrine of salvation from evil by the atonement. Also the effect of His teaching upon the race which, when truly one with His doctrine shall be in itself "The Risen Christ."

To consider all these points in detail is to fill the mind with a vivid picture of the character of Jesus Christ. To have in the mind a vivid picture of the character of Jesus Christ is to have the same mind in us that was in Him to as great extent as we realize and love that character.

It is a well-known law to metaphysical students that the mind is sure to become like the mind it associates with, whether by reading its writings or face-to-face conversations. To think much about a person or his or her characteristics is to become like him or her. A young girl thought so much about a relative who was demented that, although she prayed vehemently not to get demented, she became exactly like the relative whose character she thought upon so much.

If you think profoundly with Plato by reading his books and his life you cannot help getting polished and coldly scholarly like him with the same helpless feeling about the mastery over human experiences which he had. "We look for one," he said. What for? Why to show power over nature instead of subjection to nature like the race at large.

Suppose you looked upon the ways of Theotymus of whom St. Ambrose tells, you would certainly get willful enough to damage yourself for the sake of carrying out a sensual purpose.

"Vale lumen amicum," he said, when he found that his willfulness was destroying his eyesight. "Farewell sweet light."

If you read the book of a prejudiced mind or one that cannot keep its body well you are likely to copy the very thought that makes the bodily ailment, and soon your prejudices will be exactly like that one and your foot will be lame or your head shaking with the same palsied tremble of the one whose book you read.

Any thought is communicable. Do you know the thought that made your eyesight fail? Well, when you get hold of what it was and will drop it, your eyesight will be splendid. Jesus Christ taught the gospel of healing by keeping His doctrines and character so much in mind that other thoughts would have to fall off, and with their fall your health should "spring forth speedily."

The study of His life and ministry is the lifting of Him up in the mind. We are under orders from the Captain of our salvation to lift Him up in our minds till He draws all men unto Him. His words and character being held in mind will make us wise, strong, bold, efficient, full of health and healing love. He promised that anybody having Him supremely in mind should draw all men unto confidence in spirit — unto love of God — unto goodness of life.

This has been proved true in more ways than one. For instance, it is true of your own thoughts. If you lift Jesus Christ up, and make it your particular word, holding it steadfastly, whether it seems a reasonable thing to do or not, all the rest of your thoughts will turn towards it as flowers turn to the sun, and the drooping thought that makes you so drooping in the morning will become invigorated so that you will spring up with new life each morning.

This is the best way to effect temperance among your own thoughts and among the race of people in the world, for what an army of people could not do to put steady officers into our high seats this one name could do easily.

"Is anything too hard for Me?"

"Nay, I know not any."

By holding His name in mind and by studying the character in earnest, you will find yourself going back to Mosaic science where the proposition is made that God made everything good. Then you will see there is no power in grape juice fermented or unfermented, in tobacco plants green or dry, to do any hurt. You will see that all the sting they have is our false thoughts regarding them. That as soon as we withdraw our accusations from the things we have found growing or have manufactured from them, that they will prove their generic harmlessness.

This is the review of the year's temperance lessons. Our review is the summing up of the testimony of ideal science, which is the voluntary withdrawal on our part of the four accusations hurled by error against mankind, and caught up by the beasts of the field, the fowls of the air, and the plants of the earth.

If ever you have agreed with either of these accusations, withdraw them today and lift up the theme of this lesson. John the Revelator saw that the four angels or four thoughts of error were: first, that the children of God have lustful passions and sensual appetites; second, that they are liars; third, that they are sinners; fourth, that they are foolish and ignorant

There is one angel who stops them from hurting the people or the things of the earth. That angel is a perfect idea. Lift it up and earth is redeemed from all the stings of accusations. If you have believed any of these four evil thoughts against mankind, withdraw your accusings and refuse to believe the angels of accusing or the thoughts that are false. This is good judgment. Good judgment is temperance.

No other temperance lessons will count in demonstration.

"Jesus was born in Bethlehem of Judea in the time of Herod."

This you may take home to your own minds where your thoughts spring up. On the map of your mind there is a colony of thoughts all of the Judean quality. There is born among that herd of ideas one little thought that it is really possible to perform healing and supporting and defending by a law not material. The little sweet idea comes to you that you need not fear that any harm will come to your children or to yourself for God will take care of you. This is Jesus born in Bethlehem of Judea.

The next thought you have is the Herod one that there is no knowing what strange idiosyncrasies such a notion might lead you into. Maybe you would lose your social position or your business if this notion were allowed to grow to its full stature with you for a notion is so apt to make people peculiar; so you determine to cut off such a notion.

You cannot quite destroy it however. It is never utterly smothered in any breast, but you do relegate it to Nazareth or to the lowest place, as that only the fakirs and dervishes and mediums are miracle workers. No respectable persons do such things.

Now, miracle-working is the noblest idea you can believe in.

It is Jesus Christ. To give that idea its chance to grow within your mind would make you wise without books, strong without muscle, efficient without effort. *"No ill should come nigh thy dwelling."* Your every action would bring benefit and blessing.

You could take the common clay and make it heal blindness just as Jesus did. You remember how those other men had tried clay on the eyes of that blind man, and the clay would not work, but it worked loving healing as soon as He used it.

It is all according to the mind that uses a remedy as to whether it heals or not. The physicians have found that more depends upon the mind with which they administer doses than upon the doses. Some physicians in a certain city wondered why one of their number never lost any cases, no matter how sick they were. One of them who was highly learned in drugs went to the successful one and asked him to prescribe exactly for his cases the very same as he would for his own, which he did, and every case died, just as usual.

The mind that you hold while you cook your food or while you write your editorials heals or slays, according to what you believe. The unsuccessful physician held some idea antagonistic to Jesus. Herod ruled in his thoughts. It is healthy to believe in miracles.

Jesus, it is said, was 30 years old when He began to preach and work spiritual doctrines. So also was John. This shows that you ought to let the belief in spiritual doctrine get complete sway over your mind. One man worked 60 years to get to where he could actually feel the spirit of God present with him. The Spirit is able, ready, willing to do all things that we can ask or think of, but unless we give it complete sway we show the scars of conflict with opposition to Spirit. He taught patience by this waiting. "Patience, my heart, in loving; patience, my heart, to wait."

His whole ministry was the assurance that He might have the Kingdom of heaven right here and now. He taught the necessity for getting into the standing place of the mind, and beginning over again with a true idea of God. Everything depends upon our idea of God.

The prison houses will open when we start over the world strongly the right idea of God. The Russian starvelings will be fed if we start the true idea of God to fold the planet in. The dwarfs and old people will be straightened out with bright joyousness when the breath of our true word fans their hopeless foreheads. We made the dwarfs and the starvelings. They are our personified thoughts — our embodied false ideas of God.

You say, "I never thought of a dwarf till I saw one." Oh, no, you did not need to imagine a dwarf to make one. All you had to do was to think there are high and low, rich and poor in the universe which you have admitted God made. This will create a dwarf if you only believed it for a minute. You have only to believe that you must work and struggle to lay up for old age and feebleness, after you have once said that "the Lord will provide," to have a host of old and feeble people hanging around you.

Jesus went into the wilderness and fasted forty days to refute every false belief of the race. Fasting is simply the mortal rejection of false notions. You must learn to think for yourself quite independently of what people believe or tell you or write in books as the result of experience or observation. Unless it is good it is a lie from the beginning. Hypnotists say that as long as they can make a man think that if they tell him he is blind or lame, whether he is or not, he will act so until he rouses to think for himself, and then he is well enough.

All that we see and experience is the result of thoughts, the result of beliefs. Unless what we see is joyously good it is the product of a false idea. Fast from ideas for a while. Begin anew. This was what Jesus meant by His fast. He taught the atonement as the redemption of the world.

Atonement means at-one-ment, or at-one-mind. To be exactly of the same mind as Jesus Christ you see we have to think exactly as He did. To partake of the atonement is to find that the earthquakes could not close over us, the fires could not burn us, the water could not drown us.

These things have power over one who has not partaken of the atonement. No man passeth over this land (or over this kind of experience) and comes out alive. Only the Spirit can come up smiling and bold and unhurt when the natural forces get to working. Tottin sees that the planet is in her last throes.

"Abstract good and abstract evil are about to close in for a final conflict," he says. Once in a while all old false ideas come gathering around you and you say you have a terrible amount of sorrow and trouble. Now, if you will close your mind from thinking of your troubles and think entirely of Jesus Christ you will be lifted right up and taken over the hard place. No flesh can live where the beliefs in evil have headed. They all die unless they close their minds to the thoughts of what is going on and think of the Captain of their salvation, Jesus Christ, the righteous. When Jesus Christ was here embodied there was only Himself believing in the omnipotence of the good.

Now there are hundreds and thousands who will stand forth and sing the absoluteness of the good. Whosoever believeth and hath not doubted in his heart that God as Good is omnipresent, as

Love is omnipotent, as Spirit is omniscient, is passed from death unto life,

As the risen Christ, or risen into this faith through the gospel, we are to preach good news to all nations, beginning at Jerusalem or beginning at ourselves. We cannot do great things with the world till we have got down into the starting place of our own thoughts and got true.

"Thou must be true thyself

If thou the truth would teach."

Jonathan Edwards found out a great truth when he found that the whole purpose of God with him was to have him one with Himself.

The works would be sure to follow one who had made his peace with God.

"Acquaint now thyself with Me and be at peace." "They that understand (God) among the people shall be wise and do exploits."

December 27, 1891

.

Notes

Other Books by Emma Curtis Hopkins

- *Class Lessons of 1888 (WiseWoman Press)*
- *Bible Interpretations (WiseWoman Press)*
- *Esoteric Philosophy in Spiritual Science (WiseWoman Press)*
- *Genesis Series*
- *High Mysticism (WiseWoman Press)*
- *Self Treatments with Radiant I Am (WiseWoman Press)*
- *Gospel Series (WiseWoman Press)*
- *Judgment Series in Spiritual Science (WiseWoman Press)*
- *Drops of Gold (WiseWoman Press)*
- *Resume (WiseWoman Press)*
- *Scientific Christian Mental Practice (DeVorss)*

Books about Emma Curtis Hopkins and her teachings

- *Emma Curtis Hopkins, Forgotten Founder of New Thought –* Gail Harley
- *Unveiling Your Hidden Power: Emma Curtis Hopkins' Metaphysics for the 21st Century (also as a Workbook and as A Guide for Teachers) – Ruth L. Miller*
- *Power to Heal: Easy reading biography for all ages –Ruth Miller*

To find more of Emma's work, including some previously unpublished material, log on to:

www.emmacurtishopkins.com

WISEWOMAN PRESS

1521 NE Jantzen Ave #143
Portland, Oregon 97217
800.603.3005
www.wisewomanpress.com

Books Published by WiseWoman Press

By Emma Curtis Hopkins

- *Resume*
- *Gospel Series*
- *Class Lessons of 1888*
- *Self Treatments including Radiant I Am*
- *High Mysticism*
- *Esoteric Philosophy in Spiritual Science*
- *Drops of Gold Journal*
- *Judgment Series*
- *Bible Interpretations: series I, II and III*

By Ruth L. Miller

- *Unveiling Your Hidden Power: Emma Curtis Hopkins' Metaphysics for the 21st Century*
- *Coming into Freedom: Emily Cady's Lessons in Truth for the 21st Century*
- *150 Years of Healing: The Founders and Science of New Thought*
- *Power Beyond Magic: Ernest Holmes Biography*
- *Power to Heal: Emma Curtis Hopkins Biography*
- *The Power of Unity: Charles Fillmore Biography*
- *Uncommon Prayer*
- *Spiritual Success*
- *Finding the Path*

Watch our website for release dates and order information! - www.wisewomanpress.com

List of
Bible Interpretation Series

with date from 1st to 14th Series.

This list is complete through the fourteenth Series. Emma produced at least thirty Series of Bible Interpretations.

She followed the Bible Passages provided by the International Committee of Clerics who produced the Bible Quotations for each year's use in churches all over the world.

Emma used these for her column of Bible Interpretations in both the Christian Science Magazine, at her Seminary and in the Chicago Inter-Ocean Newspaper.

First Series

July 5 - September 27, 1891

Second Series

Third Series

Fourth Series

April 3 - June 26, 1892

Fifth Series

July 3 - September 18, 1892

Sixth Series

Seventh Series

Eighth Series

Lesson 8	Physical vs. Spiritual Power	May 21st

Lesson 8   Physical vs. Spiritual Power   May 21st
Proverbs 23:29-35
Law of Life to Elevate the Good and Banish the
Bad
Lesson Against Intemperance
Good Must Increase
To Know Goodness Is Life
The Angel of God's Presence

Lesson 9   Lesson missing   May 28th
(See Review for concept)

Lesson 10   Recognizing Our Spiritual Nature   June 4th
Proverbs 31:10-31
Was Called Emanuel
The covenant of Peace
The Ways of the Divine
Union With the Divine
Miracles Will Be Wrought

Lesson 11   Intuition   June 11th
Ezekiel 8:2-3
Ezekiel 9:3-6, 11
Interpretation of the Prophet
Ezekiel's Vision
Dreams and Their Cause
Israel and Judah
Intuition the Head
Our Limited Perspective

Lesson 12   The Book of Malachi   June 18th
Malachi
The Power of Faith
The Exercise of thankfulness
Her Faith Self-Sufficient
Burned with the Fires of Truth
What is Reality
One Open Road

Lesson 13   Review of the Quarter   June 25th
Proverbs 31:10-31

Ninth Series

July 2 - September 27, 1893

Lesson 1   Secret of all Power   July 2nd
Acts 16: 6-15   The Ancient Chinese Doctrine of Taoism
            Manifesting of God Powers
            Paul, Timothy, and Silas
            Is Fulfilling as Prophecy
            The Inner Prompting.
            Good Taoist Never Depressed
Lesson 2   The Flame of Spiritual Verity   July 9th
Acts 16:18   Cause of Contention
            Delusive Doctrines
            Paul's History
            Keynotes
            Doctrine Not New
Lesson 3   Healing Energy Gifts   July 16th
Acts 18:19-21   How Paul Healed
            To Work Miracles
            Paul Worked in Fear
            Shakespeare's Idea of Loss
            Endurance the Sign of Power
Lesson 4   Be Still My Soul   July 23rd
Acts 17:16-24   Seeing Is Believing
            Paul Stood Alone
            Lessons for the Athenians
            All Under His Power
            Freedom of Spirit
Lesson 5   (Missing) Acts 18:1-11   July 30th
Lesson 6   Missing No Lesson *   August 6th
Lesson 7   The Comforter is the Holy Ghost   August 13th
Acts 20   Requisite for an Orator
            What is a Myth
            Two Important Points
            Truth of the Gospel
            Kingdom of the Spirit
            Do Not Believe in Weakness

148

Tenth Series

October 1 – December 24, 1893

Lesson 1	*Romans 1:1-19*	October 1st

When the Truth is Known
Faith in God
The Faithful Man is Strong
Glory of the Pure Motive

Lesson 2	*Romans 3:19-26*	October 8th

Free Grace.
On the Gloomy Side
Daniel and Elisha
Power from Obedience
Fidelity to His Name
He Is God

Lesson 3	*Romans 5*	October 15th

The Healing Principle
Knows No Defeat.
In Glorified Realms
He Will Come

Lesson 4	*Romans 12:1*	October 22nd

Would Become Free
Man's Co-operation
Be Not Overcome
Sacrifice No Burden
Knows the Future

Lesson 5	*I Corinthians 8:1-13*	October 29th

The Estate of Man
Nothing In Self
What Paul Believed
Doctrine of Kurozumi

Lesson 6	*I Corinthians 12:1-26*	November 5th

Science of The Christ Principle
Dead from the Beginning
St. Paul's Great Mission
What The Spark Becomes
Chris, All There Is of Man
Divinity Manifest in Man
Christ Principle Omnipotent

150

Eleventh Series

Twelfth Series

Thirteenth Series

July 1 – September 30, 1894

Lesson 1   The Birth of Jesus   July 1st
Luke 2:1-16
No Room for Jesus
Man's Mystic Center
They glorify their Performances

Lesson 2   Presentation in the Temple   July 8th
Luke 2:25-38
A Light for Every Man
All Things Are Revealed
The Coming Power
Like the Noonday Sun

Lesson 3   Visit of the Wise Men   July 15th
Matthew 1:2-12
The Law Our Teacher
Take neither Scrip nor Purse
The Star in the East
The Influence of Truth

Lesson 4   Flight Into Egypt   July 22nd
Mathew 2:13-23
The Magic Word of Wage Earning
How Knowledge Affect the Times
The Awakening of the Common People

Lesson 5   The Youth of Jesus   July 29th
Luke2:40-52
Your Righteousness is as filthy Rags
Whatsoever Ye Search, that will Ye Find
The starting Point of All Men
Equal Division, the Lesson Taught by Jesus
The True Heart Never Falters

Lesson 6   The "All is God" Doctrine   August 5th
Luke 2:40-52
Three Designated Stages of Spiritual Science
Christ Alone Gives Freedom
The Great Leaders of Strikes

Lesson 7   Missing   August 12th

Lesson 8   First Disciples of Jesus   August 19th
John 1:36-49
The Meaning of Repentance

Fourteenth Series

CPSIA information can be obtained
at www.ICGtesting.com
Printed in the USA
FSOW04n0914190515
7268FS

9 780945 385523